Many Paths,
One Truth

Many Paths, One Truth

An Affirmation of Spirit

Rev. Barry King, PhD(TC), OM

Illustrated by P. John Burden

iUniverse, Inc.
Bloomington

MANY PATHS, ONE TRUTH
An Affirmation of Spirit

iUniverse books may be ordered through booksellers or by contacting:

iUniverse
1663 Liberty Drive
Bloomington, IN 47403
www.iuniverse.com
1-800-Authors (1-800-288-4677)

ISBN: 978-1-4759-6983-2 (sc)
ISBN: 978-1-4759-6984-9 (ebk)

Printed in the United States of America

iUniverse rev. date: 01/21/2013

Acknowledgments

As I have moved along my path, I have been blessed with the guidance and support of a number of very special people. Although it is possible to mention only a few, my gratitude goes out to all those I have met along my journey.

First, I would like to thank my mother and father for their love and support over the years. They did not always understand me but they did always offer me their unconditional love and guidance. I am grateful for having such wonderful parents who provided me with such a loving model to emulate.

I would like to thank Elizabeth Canning for introducing me to the Spiritual Science Fellowship Interfaith Ministry. Thank you to Rev. Dr. Frederick Cale who guided and nurtured me (and still does from the Spirit World) as I move along the path of service within the Ministry. Thank you to Rev. Dr. Marilyn Rossner, founder of the S.S.F. Interfaith Ministry whose vision and compassion has touched so many souls. Through the guidance and example of these three people, I have learned the path of inclusiveness, service and Light.

As I look at this book, I am also grateful for the illustrations that P. John Burden has provided which translate my words into such wonderful images. Thank you, John.

And finally, I would like to thank my wife, Rev. Dr. Sandi, whose love and support has made so much possible. Through Sandi, I have been blessed with not only a life-partner who shares my love and joy of service to Spirit but also an angel who reminds me that we are all part of the one Light.

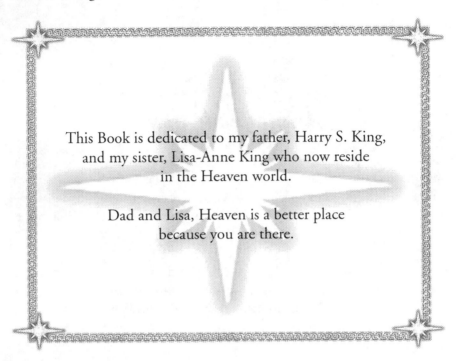

This Book is dedicated to my father, Harry S. King,
and my sister, Lisa-Anne King who now reside
in the Heaven world.

Dad and Lisa, Heaven is a better place
because you are there.

Preface

The foundation of this book is made up of inspirational writings/talks that I have shared at our Interfaith Services. Because of this, at times you might find some repetition.

I have included in the book some additional elements which I thought you might enjoy. One of these elements is called "Spirit Speaks." It contains information channelled from Spirit by me during some of our regular channelling sessions. Another element I have included is called "On Angel's Wings." These are true stories shared by real people which illustrate the power of Spirit to transform lives. Also included are excerpts from the World's Sacred Texts which express the interfaith perspective.

Experiences with Spirit can be subtle or profound. Transformational experiences with Spirit can include prayers answered, miraculous happenings, out-of-body experiences, contact by departed loved ones, near-death experiences, and many more. If you have experiences you would like to share send your story to us at 32 Greenwood Drive, Charlottetown, Prince Edward Island, Canada, C1C 1J3 or visit our website at www. Interfaithministry.com and send us a message.

I wish you Peace, Joy and Many Bright Blessings,
Rev. Barry King, Ph.D.(TC)

Contents

Introduction

I have been sensitive to the world of Spirit since I was a child. This means that I was not only blessed and supported by two wonderful parents but that I had the added benefit of my connection to the Divine Source through Spirit. This connection was not always welcomed since I learned very quickly that everyone did not share my ability to see the unseen world. This ability made me different and, in time, I learned to repress it or at least hide it.

It was only when Spirit introduced me to Elizabeth Canning, a gifted medium/intuitive, that my spiritual journey became focused and my gifts awakened. Elizabeth introduced me to the Spiritual Science Fellowship and it was there that I felt I had come home. Here I found a community of people who understood Spirit and embraced an interfaith perspective with integrity and love. I had chosen a path of service and, with the Fellowship, I had a vehicle through which I could serve those who wished to explore their own spirituality and the world of Spirit.

After a number of years working and studying in the Spiritual Science Fellowship Interfaith Ministry, my wife Sandi and I founded the Prince Edward Island (PEI) Interfaith Ministry and then the Open International Interfaith Ministry (OIIM) and the iNtuitive Times Institute, the Ministry's four year seminary program. For more than twenty-five years I have had the pleasure of working with Spirit in the Interfaith Ministry. From the beginning, I was blessed with the guidance and support of Rev. Frederick Cale, Ph.D. in Halifax. I am eternally grateful for his patience and willingness to share his experience and wisdom with me. He was my friend and mentor as I moved along the path to the Ministry. And even though he made his transition into the Spirit realm a number of years ago, I know he continues to work with me from the Spirit World.

When I started on this journey of service, I found that there was very little written to act as a guide or road map when working in an Interfaith context. I found there was nothing that consolidated all the points of view into a context that could help our members understand clearly and simply who we were as people following an Interfaith faith path and what this meant in terms of how we understood the Divine and perceived Spirit.

For many years, we have operated regular Services of Worship for our members in Prince Edward Island. These services are structured to be a celebration of God and God's gifts in our lives. A regular element of each service is the lecture. Upon looking at a number of these short inspirational talks, it occurred to me that these talks could be used as a foundation to understand the interfaith perspective, as well as, act as an introduction to the Interfaith Ministry. This book consists of a number of these inspirational talks. For those who cannot get to our services or who would like to know a little about how we perceive God and the Spirit realms, this book will provide some insight. Please forgive any repetition you might find in these pages. Each of the talks is written to stand alone so some important points or principles may be repeated.

I have included a few of my own personal experiences and proofs in the lectures to illustrate particular points. It is important, however, that each of us develop our own personal proofs to testify to the reality of God in our lives. Even though the experiences of others can act to illustrate what is possible, an understanding of Spirit must be developed from within. Your relationship with God is a personal one and, therefore, it is only through experience that we develop an absolute sense of the reality of Spirit and Spirit phenomena.

The lectures that I share with you embrace my understanding of Spirit and although I believe it is representative, it is by no means meant to be a total synthesis of all that is within the Interfaith Ministry and its faith path. How humanity as a people understands God and the manifestations of Spirit in the world is diverse with foundations in the cultural and individual identities of people all over the earth.

The more that I work with Spirit and Spirit/psychic phenomena, the clearer it becomes to me that all things are possible. This means that just as we are infinite and eternal as Spirit, so are the potential manifestations of Spirit in the physical world infinite. When "thoughts are things", all things have the potential to take form and manifest if given enough energy. That is why what we think and how we think is so important. Our thoughts have the power to shape and mould the world we live in.

The other thing I should explain is what I mean by the word "*Spirit.*" When I use the term "*Spirit*" with a capital "*S*", I am speaking of God—the Divine Essence and all those who serve God. That includes angels, Spirit guides, Spirit workers, our loved ones, etc.—all of whom choose to serve God by serving us. Even in the Heaven world, those in the spirit realms can grow and learn and move closer to the Divine by accomplishing God's work. One of the tasks open to those on the other side is working with souls who are immersed in the physical and who need support and guidance.

I am a Spirit encased in a physical body. As Spirit, I have a number of natural gifts that I have inherited. These gifts include clairvoyance, clairaudience, clairsentience, aura sensing, prophecy, divination, healing and others. You are also Spirit and have been given these gifts. They are as natural as taking a breath of clean fresh air. To some, psychic gifts come easier than to others. We all have gifts and everyone is psychic. We all have the ability to work with the unseen world. *It is natural because we are Spirit.*

As we are all souls, people who have developed their psychic abilities are not necessarily spiritual. A spiritual person will use their "psychic" or "soul gifts" through love and through service. It is important to understand that these psychic gifts can be perverted and used to serve the negative. Psychic gifts, not used through love, can be used to control and manipulate people and events. They can be used to gain wealth and power. This does not mean that psychic gifts are evil or negative. It does mean that people must choose how they use their gifts. Free will gives us the choice to use our gifts to serve the Light or the darkness.

I cannot believe in the traditional Christian perception of hell. I do not believe that people go to a place called hell where they are damned for all time. The most obvious thing to me is that God loves us all unconditionally. Damnation is a tool of fear and anger. Damnation is not a tool of love. God—the Divine provides us all with as many opportunities as we need to make the right choices and grow in love. No matter what you have been taught, someday we will all stand in the Heaven World together as brothers and sisters.

For me, the belief in our ability to grow spiritually in understanding depends on the acceptance of the idea that we can choose to have more than one lifetime in the physical. If we did not, we would not have the opportunity to correct our mistakes, make amends or express what we have learned through action. It is only through our time in this great classroom that we are now in, that we can experience the challenges of a physical existence.

The belief in reincarnation is as old as religion itself. It is more widely accepted by the Eastern religions than the West. The belief is especially central to Hinduism. The Hindu Scriptures, such as the *Upanishads* and *Bhagavad Gita*, refer pointedly to reincarnation. The *Gita* notes:

> *"As leaving aside worn-out garments*
> *A man takes other, new ones,*
> *So leaving aside worn-out bodies*
> *To other, new ones goes the embodied (soul)."*

I particularly like the way that Benjamin Franklin expressed his belief in reincarnation and the purposefulness of life when he had the following inscribed on his tombstone:

> *"The body of B. Franklin Printer,*
> *Like the cover of an old book,*
> *Its contents torn out and*

Stripped of its lettering & gilding lies here
But the book shall not be lost,
For it will as he believed appear once more
In a new and more elegant edition
Revised and corrected by the author."

I believe that life is purposeful and that we grow and become aware through our choices in life made both from the physical and from the Spirit realms.

I do believe, however, that if you feel that you deserve to go to hell, you may wake up on the other side in a place that very much resembles it. Thoughts are things in Spirit and if you believe in hell, you can create it. You will move into the higher realms when you realize that it is only your thoughts which hold you back. When we make the transition into Spirit, we judge ourselves and we experience all the pain we have caused others in life.

When in the Spirit realm, we do not become instantly wise. Since like attracts like and we are vibrational by nature, we can be drawn to a place where we are surrounded by those who share the vibration we had in life. This means that if a soul was greedy and intolerant and has not chosen to let go of those qualities during their transition into Spirit, they will go to a place which is between the physical world and the Heaven world where they will be surrounded by people who are greedy and intolerant. This will not be a pleasant place because it is dark and full of negativity. Here the soul will remain until it realizes that it is there because of the way he/she has chosen to think. Once this process has begun and the soul begins to reject the negative qualities, ministering Spirits will appear to escort him/her to a place of learning where the soul can continue its journey into the higher vibrations. Progress is always a matter of choice and no one is ever forsaken.

In closing, I would like to thank you for allowing me to share with you. It can be very difficult trying to translate non-physical or Spiritual concepts into the concrete. What is most amazing about things relating to Spirit is their simplicity. I pray that Spirit has helped me to reflect this simplicity and to achieve clarity in the pages which follow.

I hope you enjoy this book as much as I have enjoyed writing it. I hope that it encourages you to think about your connection to the God of your understanding and that it helps you to grow in your understanding of Spirit. May it bring you peace and joy and help you move further along your personal spiritual path.

In God's Love and Light,
Rev. Barry King, Ph.D.

Prayer of Saint Francis

Make me a channel of your peace.
Where there is hatred, let me bring your love.
Where there is injury, your pardon Lord.
And where there is doubt, true faith in you.

Make me a channel of your peace.
Where there is despair in life, let me bring hope.
Where there is darkness, only light.
Where there is sadness ever joy.

Oh, Master grant that I may never seek
So much to be consoled as to console.
To be understood as to understand.
To be loved, as to love, with all my soul.

Make me a channel of your peace.
It is in pardoning that we are pardoned.
In giving to all people, we receive,
And in dying that we're born to eternal life.

The Paths are Many, the Truth is One.

Confucius said . . . "In the world there are many different roads but the destination is the same. There are a hundred deliberations but the result is one."
Confucianism.
I Ching, Appended Remarks 2.5

As men approach Me, so I receive them. All paths, Arjuna, lead to Me.
Hinduism.
Bhagavad Gita 4.11

Say, "We believe in God, and in what has been revealed to us, and what was revealed to Abraham, Ishmael, Isaac, Jacob, and the Tribes, and in what was given to Moses, Jesus, and the Prophets from their Lord. We make no distinction between any of them, and to God do we submit."
Islam.
Qur'an 3.84t

God is a God of Diversity

As Interfaith Ministers, it is natural for us to approach spirituality from an interfaith perspective. That means that our approach is inclusive celebrating all traditions and diverse approaches to spiritual practice. When we look at the beautiful, diverse world that God has created for us, it is clear to us that God is a God of diversity. There is not just one type of tree, or one type of bird, or one type of flower, or one type of person. The world is populated with a multitude of forms which are trees, and birds, and flowers, and people in all shapes, sizes and colours. This diversity makes the world more beautiful.

If we believe that God is infinite, then one place to begin to understand God is to embrace the knowledge that in this diverse and beautiful world created by God, it is only natural that God should manifest the message of unconditional love in many ways to many peoples. There is one God but it is a God of many faces. We, in the Interfaith Ministry, celebrate these many faces of God represented by different religious and spiritual traditions and rejoice that we have been given such a beautiful and diverse world. We express this truth with the phrase, "The paths are many, the truth is one. Love thy neighbour."

You Are a Force for Whatever You Believe!

You probably don't realize it, but you are changing the world. And the truth is you are changing it because that is what you are supposed to do. We live in a purposeful universe. In such a universe, each of us has his or her role to play. You may think, "How can I change the world?" Well you already have. Look around you. You are a force for whatever you believe and as such you're making a difference. It's also true that because it is a purposeful universe, you have free will. That means that you have the choice to be either a positive force or a negative force. It's important for each of us to understand that we have an impact on the world—the world around us—the world within us—the world beyond us.

The more I have worked with Spirit, the clearer it has become to me that we live in the world of our own creation. We are like-minded souls working together changing the world. The question that begs to be asked is "What kind of world do we want to live in?" The physical world is "heavier" and much harder to shape than the world of Spirit. Because of this heavy vibration it is also easy sometimes for us to get bogged down in physicality and negative emotions. We forget that even though we are at this moment in a physical world, we are limitless, infinite, and open to a world of possibilities.

Over the years, I have been blessed with the opportunity to not only work with Spirit but also to experience the boundless possibilities of an infinite universe. We are only just beginning to understand how powerful our thoughts are and the reality that all things in an infinite universe are possible.

As you embrace your heritage as a living soul, you will enter a new world of awareness. I welcome you to the world of Spirit. It is a diverse but simple world guided by gentle and loving principles. It is a world of personal responsibility and of wonderful connectedness. It is a world of possibilities—a world of the miraculous—a world of challenge. Those who enter this world will be challenged through loving purposefulness to become all they can be. It is a timeless world where all things are possible and happen in their time.

I believe that each of us must develop our own personal proof to testify to the reality of God in our lives. Even though the experiences of others can act to illustrate what is possible, an understanding of the nature of Spirit can only be truly developed from within. Your relationship with God is a personal one, and therefore, it is only through personal experience that you develop an absolute sense of the reality of Spirit and Spirit phenomena.

As Spirit, we have a number of natural gifts that we have inherited. These gifts including clairvoyance (clear seeing), clairaudience (clear hearing), clairsentience (clear feeling), prophecy, divination, spiritual healing and many other special perceptions of the spiritual mind are natural to us all. To some in the physical, expressing and experiencing these gifts is easier than for others; just as the ability to play a piano or do math comes easier to some. Everyone is psychic. It is natural because we are Spirit and we are infinite.

The word psychic comes from the Greek word for "soul." Psychic gifts are, therefore, "soul gifts." Even though the word psychic and the use of psychic gifts have been perverted over the years by those wishing to control others, the positive use of your soul gifts acknowledges your birthright as an eternal soul. Psychic gifts used through love are by nature positive, healing, creative and constructive.

Twenty-five years ago, when I started in the Ministry, the idea of an Interfaith community and the notion of a personal connection to Spirit was a mystery to most and an affront to some. Today, it is gratifying to see that there has been a positive change towards embracing diversity and towards people following a personal expression of spirituality. The days of fire and brimstone are waning and being replaced with loving intent towards a more universal understanding of our source—our God essence.

There is, however, still much to do. One of the reasons I dedicated myself to the Interfaith Ministry was because of the intolerance and misunderstanding of other spiritual paths that I saw in some faith communities. This intolerance meant there were loving souls who worshipped the God of their understanding and because of this, they lived in fear. These people lived in fear because their faith had taken them along a different path. They were persecuted because they understood God differently. These people could be you or me. They loved their children. They were kind, considerate and lived on the whole a spiritual life. If we have learned anything it should be that enough wars have been fought in the name of God's Love and that enough souls have suffered at the hands of those who would "save" them because they are different. The message of an Interfaith Ministry is a simple one, "The paths are many, the truth is one—love thy neighbour." Look within yourself. If you find that you are intolerant or uncertain of other ways, take the time to learn about them—to understand them. All approaches to spiritual practice which have at their core the "God Essence" and loving intent are worthy of our respect and support.

It seems inconceivable to me that people should suffer because they worship and love God. It is sad that some souls feel that they need to fear God or that they need to instill in others a fear of God. I believe that to fear God is to pervert a basic truth:

"GOD IS LOVE."

I am pleased to say that the notion of an Interfaith community is much more acceptable today than it was when I began. It is true that many people still have a difficult time understanding how a Ministry can exist which embraces all traditions. The Interfaith Ministry—the Interfaith Faith Path—celebrates the ceremony, symbols and articulations of

God's message of love through all traditions. It should also be noted that we encourage our members to reject that which is grounded in the physical such as fear, intolerance, greed, hatred and prejudice. These are by nature not spiritual qualities and should have no place in spiritual practice.

One of the challenges of the interfaith perspective is to build a sense of community when each faith component of that community potentially sees itself as exclusive or ultimately right. An example is the use of the term "Interfaith" to define an inter-denominational Christian congregation. For us, the Interfaith community is by definition a multi-faith community bringing together people from all faiths and traditions to celebrate the many faces of God. The goal of the Interfaith Path must help people understand that loving souls, no matter what their faith, are equal in the eyes of God and will stand together in the world of Spirit.

Many Interfaith Ministers are also Ministers within a more traditional belief system. Since we are interfaith in perspective, we encourage participation by persons from all faiths and traditions. At any Interfaith meeting or service, you could find Christian Priests, Ministers, Jewish Rabbis, Hindu Swamis, Sikhs, Buddhists Lamas, Jain Monks, Spiritualist Ministers, Native Medicine Men and others sharing the platform. Many people attending Interfaith services and activities bring to it their connection to their own faith and traditions and continue to participate in their traditional faith. Others, however, see the Interfaith Ministry as their spiritual practice and approach the Interfaith Ministry as the faith path they want to follow.

Mystical experiences are the validating foundation of most religions and act as proof of a greater reality. Over the years it has also become quite clear to me that many, if not most people, have had experiences which they cannot explain through their understanding of the physical world. These experiences can be defined as spiritual, psychic or intuitive and are difficult to reproduce on demand or to clearly articulate using language. Such experiences are the foundation of all religious traditions and experience yet they are not considered valid unless performed by the "faithful." They are miraculous by nature and are too often filed away within our consciousness as experiences that cannot be shared because people do not understand them or because people will not accept them. To many people in today's technological information-based world, there is the belief that if it cannot be understood or analyzed then it cannot exist. This misconception should be easily dispelled by scientists working with such concepts as "Chaos Theory" and "Quantum Physics." Theories such as Einstein's theory of relativity are changing as we develop a greater understanding of the laws which guide the universe. Einstein's theory states that nothing can move faster than the speed of light. Today researchers have now measured speeds of up to 10 times the speed of light in some atomic particles. They have also found that some particles are moving so fast that they defy the laws of time and actually arrive at the location before they left. Time travel is a reality!

It is true that our busy pace and our total immersion in the physical separates us from our connections to the spiritual dimensions from which we originated. We, in an Interfaith community, are able to validate Spirit-based experiences and help provide a structure through which people can understand them. One day a lady called and asked if she could speak to me. She explained that she had been having a very unsettling experience she did not understand. She was embarrassed to talk about it but it had happened a number of times and she hoped that I would understand. She said that she would be sitting in the chair in her living room and all of a sudden would find herself drifting outside the window (she lived on the tenth floor) looking in at her body. She would panic because not only did she not know how she got there but she did not know how she could get back. A few minutes later she would find herself back in her body feeling quite exhausted. She had talked to her minister about it and a priest and they had told her that she was imagining things and should talk to a psychiatrist. She had originally thought that maybe she was going crazy but the only manifestation of the "illness" was these experiences and she felt there must be another answer. After we talked for a while, she felt much better. I explained to her the nature of spontaneous astral projection (soul spontaneously leaves the physical body) and how she could return to her body with merely a thought. Not only was it reassuring to her to have someone who could relate to the experience, but it was also important that we were able to empower her to do something about it. She did not have to be a victim of her special gift. One of the first steps to understanding something is accepting its reality.

Another reason for my commitment to the Interfaith Ministry was my awareness of the world of Spirit from a very young age. I have always been sensitive to the world of Spirit. As a child, I remember a small white ball of light which would float just above a day couch in my room and sing to me at night. The singing was in a woman's voice and was the most beautiful, calming sound. Today, I know the light was an angel and the singing was an angel's voice. I can still hear it in my mind today.

I also remember when I was 5 or 6 years of age that I would go to sleep at night and wake up in a place where the kindest and gentlest people would talk to me and show me around. They looked beautiful and healthy and were filled with light and joy. I remember them taking me by the hand and walking me through gardens and gatherings of people. While I was visiting, I was conscious that my physical body was back in the bed asleep. Even though everyone was very nice, I would try to make my body wake up because I knew I was not supposed to be talking to dead people (people in Spirit). In time, I trained myself not to have (or at least not to remember) these experiences.

I still have vivid memories of those excursions into the Heaven World. It is important to know that I was not aware that everyone was not having these experiences. They were normal to me and I assumed they were normal to everyone. It was only as I grew older that I became aware that the experiences I was having were considered unusual. I had to wait until I became an adult and found the Interfaith Ministry before I was able to allow my gifts to manifest in a meaningful way.

To me the reality of the Spiritual realms and of God is not a matter of faith but is an absolute truth based on personal experience. I have been blessed with experiences whose foundations in the physical world allow me to testify with absolute assurance that we are immortal and that God moves in each of our lives. I would like to share with everyone the wonderful feeling of standing with a foot in both worlds. I am here to tell you that no one is ever lost from the heart of God and that each of us in our own way, in our own time, will know and understand our spiritual heritage. We are all spiritual beings. We are all psychic and connected to Spirit. Unfortunately, many of us reject our natural connections and our birthright to the Spirit realms as we become immersed in the physical world and modern society.

A few years ago a good friend of mine who is a medium made an observation which had particular meaning to me. He noted that there are many Spirit worlds and that in reality we are living in one today. He noted that when we make our transition, it is like stepping through a door and in reality the Spirit World we move into does not seem that different. That is because the physical world, even though it is not made of the finer vibrations of the higher realms, is a vibrational world and as such is a Spirit world. As a Spirit world, it is subject to a number of basic laws.

I do not believe in the devil. That doesn't mean that I don't accept that there is negativity and wickedness in the world. I do believe there are negative entities who gather their strength from the negative emotions which exist in the physical world such as greed, hate, and fear. I believe, however, that to fear these entities is to give them power. To think about them with anything other than pity is to feed them. To overcome negativity, surround yourself with love and know that this power of love is absolute in the universe. It dispels all negativity as surely as light dispels darkness. The darkness cannot exist in the Light. Evil and negativity cannot exist in an environment of love and positive thought. When we teach people to fear evil and negativity, we teach them to call it to them and give it strength.

I believe that we live in a vibrational universe and that our physical body's vibration corresponds to the vibration of the physical universe we live in. It can also be said that our soul vibration is a reflection of our spiritual growth and achievement. This means that when we make our transition and leave our physical body, we will find ourselves placed vibrationally with like-minded souls. If we are hateful and mean-spirited, when we make our transition into the Spirit realm, we will find ourselves surrounded by hateful and mean-spirited souls until we learn to let go of those negative qualities. If we are, as most people are, inherently positive, then we will move to the higher Heaven world.

Understand that your thoughts have a great deal to do with where you go when you make your transition. There is a place in the Heaven World—a simple place where a group of people live who have a fundamental belief that they are the chosen ones of God. They believe that all those who do not follow their faith path in life cannot enter the world of Heaven. Their Heaven is a very small place. It has flowers and trees, a small church, nice houses, fields, beautiful skies, but it is home for only a few. These people have limited themselves and closed themselves off from a greater truth. They do not know the infinite glory of the true Heaven World. Every so often someone disappears from their Heaven—someone who has embraced and understood the greater truth—that God is Love and that all are Children of the Light. There are always new people to take their place.

The vast multitudes of souls living in the Heaven World move past this small place, limited by the beliefs of those who live there, quietly looking in with sadness—for these people have cut themselves off from the glorious, beautiful and diverse Heaven that the vast majority of loving souls know. Even in the Heaven World, we can be prisoners of our awareness.

The good news is that even those who are filled by negative thought forms and emotions and who find themselves in the lower astral planes will eventually choose to move to the higher realms as their awareness grows and they reject negativity. Everyone is provided with all the opportunities they need to choose love and to progress. No matter what you have been taught, some day we will all stand in the Heaven World together as brothers and sisters.

Keeping in mind the fact that we are now living in a Spirit World, I would like to share with you a few basic laws and thoughts relating to the nature of Spirit and the world that we live in.

God is a God of diversity. There is not just one type of tree, or one type of bird, or one type of flower, or one type of person. The world is populated with a multitude of forms which are trees, and birds, and flowers, and people in all shapes, sizes and colour. This diversity makes the world more beautiful. Creation is infinite, incomprehensible and wondrous.

It is important to note that thoughts are things. Thoughts, if given enough energy, will become manifest. Another way of saying this is, "As you think, so it is." Therefore, if you believe the world is an unfriendly place, it will be. It is also true that if you believe the world is full of joy, you will find joy at every turn. What do you choose?

The world of Spirit is a world of thought. Thoughts in the higher Spirit realms are immediately manifested. If you wish to live in a great mansion, you will. If you wish to travel to other planets and see miraculous sights, you will.

In the physical, thoughts also become things but it is a slower and more tedious process. The chair you are sitting in was once a thought form and now it has been translated into the physical. The physical is made of much slower vibrations than that of Spirit so it takes more energy and effort to manifest. Things in the physical must be shaped and moulded, but be assured, the world you live in is the product of your thoughts—both the negative and the positive.

The Spiritual path is a path of challenges. When you step onto the spiritual path, you are saying to the God of your understanding, "Challenge me!" You have chosen the circumstances you were born into. They provided you with the best potential to learn and experience the things that you have chosen to experience in this life. It is only in the physical that one can experience the things of the physical such as pain, suffering, loss, grief, frustration, etc. It is not what you go through in this life which moves you forward along the path but what you choose to do with it.

Everything happens for a reason. Life is purposeful. In some ways, you can never make a mistake. Everything you do has consequences and those consequences provide us with opportunities to learn. If you have made a choice which has moved you into an unpleasant consequence, then learning from it will hopefully mean that you will not make the same choice again. If you have not learned from the experience, you will have another opportunity. Every choice moves you forward along your path, your spiritual journey.

You are measured not by your deeds but by your thoughts. If you do good things because you feel you have to or will be punished if you don't, then from the point of view of our spiritual growth, what is the value of doing those good things? Things must be done because they are right, not because you are afraid. It is your intention that defines what you do. It is your intent which is measured and evaluated when it comes time for you to look at your life from the Spirit realm and judge your progress. So even though you may have a lifetime of apparently good deeds, you may not reap the benefits of those deeds if they were done through greed, or fear, or the need for power or control. It is your intention which matters.

Remember that every thought is a prayer. It is not only when you call a thought a prayer that God—the Universe listens. God hears your thoughts whether you are officially praying or not. As mentioned earlier, treat every thought as if it will become a reality. That means that when you have a negative thought, you must learn to transform it into a positive. Today is not a difficult day—"Today is a wonderful day to be alive. Thank you for the challenges which have provided me with the opportunity to grow." Affirmations are important because they work. "*Every thought is a thing.*"

You do not have a soul, you are a soul. Even though you are housed in a physical body, you are not a physical entity. You are eternal and of Spirit.

You have the gift of free will. We have been given the opportunity to choose our path and to make mistakes and to grow. We live in a universe of free choice. God does not make choices for us and there is no devil to blame our actions on. We choose. We make mistakes. We learn. We grow.

In closing, I say to you support those servants of the Light who walk along a different path. Support those who have a different colour or vibration but serve the Divine—the God of their understanding and bring love and joy into the world. How will you recognize them? They will know that they are not perfect and that they are not in possession of an exclusive truth. They will work through love and not fear or hate. They will seek and not reject truths which force them to re-examine their understanding of the world.

Truth seekers from all faiths who reject fear are your brothers and sisters. They rejoice in the knowledge that others have found God's Light through another path. Rejoice in the knowledge that the joy and love in your heart is of the Light and that you one day will stand with your brothers and sisters from all faiths together in the world of Spirit.

On Death

When I was very young (about 11 or 12), I wrote a poem. Amazingly, I still remember it. It was titled, "Death" and I would like to share it with you.

Death

The Question is unanswered,
But pondered by us all.
For Death it hath dominion
For all men have to fall.

The Silver cord is severed.
The soul is free at last.
The future now awaits you,
Man's soul can feel no past.

Today, I feel differently about this question and the answer. I know with absolute certainty that there is no death. The physical body does indeed die, but the soul, however, is eternal and continues forever. The death of the physical body is like the opening of a door. Through this door you step from this world into the next. Not only does your memory and the essence of the individual remain intact, but in time you will regain the memories which were lost in the transition into the physical.

The evidence to support this is experiential. I have been given a gift, which allows me the opportunity to communicate with and see those on the other side of the door we know as death. I have had many proofs of the existence of a life beyond this life. My answers today come from personal experience and confirmations of those experiences I have had while I have been here in the physical. I have been blessed with the opportunity to do tens of thousands of readings over the years. Each reading brings me a new confirmation to the reality of the Spirit realms and of the absolute truth of our continued existence and awareness after the change called death.

Below are a few examples of experiences I have had with people who have come to see me. It is important to remember that for the most part these experiences are spontaneous. When people come to see me, I do not know them or why they have come to see me. I have learned to trust that Spirit knows why they have come and will address the issues at hand.

One night we were doing a meditation and development group which included messages from Spirit. The father of one of the participants arrived and had a message he wanted to share with his daughter. The man was in Spirit and had been there for a number of years. The daughter wanting some confirmation that this was indeed her father asked how he had died. The man told me that he had died after he had fallen down the stairs. This was early in my career of working with those in Spirit and for some reason, I did not believe him. I told the father that he would have to give me another answer. Somewhat surprised, the Spirit said, "Well, you can tell her that I had a heart attack." I shared this answer with the woman. She looked puzzled and said to me, "I suppose that could be the reason why he fell down the stairs." I learned an important lesson that night. I had robbed this woman of her proof. I had not trusted the message I had received.

Another time, I was doing a public demonstration. As I looked into the audience, I saw a woman from Spirit appear beside her daughter. I told the woman that her mother was there and that as proof that it was her, she was showing me her hair which was perfect and her feet which seemed to be causing her lots of difficulty. The woman laughing said,

"That's mom OK. She had her hair done every Friday and it was always perfect. Her feet caused her lots of trouble in life because she had worn high heels and in her later years she had developed bunions."

A year or so ago, I was doing a message circle with eleven people from a local community each who had lost someone for whom they were grieving. Even though I did not know whom they had lost or the circumstances, each received a message from the person that they were hoping to connect with.

For example, when I connected to one lady in the group (Joanne), a young woman appeared. I described the young woman in Spirit to Joanne. She was showing me her pierced ears which had two piercings in each ear. She wanted me to tell Joanne that she was fine and that she was not upset with her. She was happy and comfortable on the Spirit-side and wanted Joanne to stop feeling guilty and to know that she loved her. The message continued for a while and Joanne was clearly moved and tearful.

After the young woman from Spirit had left, Joanne explained that this had been her daughter and that she had died in a car accident about six months previously. The evening that she had died she had come home with her ears pierced with two piercings in each ear earlier in the day. They had argued about it and her daughter had left the house angry. That was the last time she had seen her daughter alive. Joanne had been haunted by the fact that her last words had been ones of anger and that she had not told her daughter that she had loved her when she left the house that last time. Every person that evening got a message from their loved one in Spirit that was healing and validated that they were alive and well on the Spirit side.

It may be surprising to realize that those on the Spirit side can do the things they enjoyed in life in the Heaven world. For example, a woman came to see me in my office a few weeks ago. She was clearly troubled and when I connected to her, her husband who had made his transition recently into the Heaven World showed up. He was quite a character and quite a pleasant fellow. I said to the woman that he must have loved horses. I could see him somewhere sitting watching the horse races. She said laughing, *"That would be him. He loved the races and raised horses on the farm."* I said to her that he was also showing me a deck of cards and seemed to be playing cards with a group of friends. Again she laughed saying, *"The only thing he loved more than horses was playing cards."* The session went on for about 40 minutes. I could see a great weight taken off her as she left knowing that her husband was alive and well in Spirit.

For me, after many years of working with Spirit in very concrete ways, there is certainty that we are eternal and that there is no death.

In the Bible, we read of the two bodies—the physical and the spiritual; the mortal and the immortal.

In Corinthians 1: Chapter 15 *Verses 42-44*

> *So will it be with the resurrection of the dead. The body that is sown is perishable; it is sown in dishonour, it is raised in glory; it is sown in weakness, it is raised in power. It is sown a natural body; it is raised a Spiritual body. If there is a natural body, there is also a Spiritual body.*

Verses 51-55

> *Listen, I tell you a mystery: We will not all sleep but we will all be changed—in a flash, in a twinkling of an eye, at the last trumpet. For the trumpet will sound, the dead will be raised imperishable, and we will be changed. For the perishable must clothe itself with the imperishable, and the mortal with immortality.*

> *When the perishable has been clothed in the imperishable, and the mortal with immortality, then the saying that is written will come true. "Death has been swallowed up in victory."*

> *"Where O death, is your victory? Where O death is your sting?"*

Psychics, shaman, and Spiritualists have always known of the two bodies—the physical and the etheric—the mortal body and the soul.

It is difficult sometimes, immersed in a physical body, to recognize that we are Spiritual beings. It is not that you have a soul; it is that you *are* a soul. You are eternal and you are of God. Your physical body is merely the container in which you have housed yourself for this lifetime on earth. You are a spiritual being choosing to experience a physical life.

It is also difficult for us to understand how it works. How can the physical and Spirit realms interpenetrate each other? How can a Spirit body take up residence in a physical body?

Imagine for a moment that our states of existence are like water. Water molecules at different rates of vibration create water in different forms. When the molecules are vibrating slowly, they create ice. When the water molecules are vibrating very fast, they create water vapour. Between these two, we have liquid water which is an intermediary.

Our physical world has a slow vibration and can be likened to ice. It is not easily malleable. It is heavy and sometimes difficult to work with. Ice cannot penetrate ice because it shares a common vibration.

Our Spiritual bodies have a very fast vibration and can be likened to water vapour. In this high vibrational state our Spirit bodies are light, intangible, energetic, and malleable. This is the nature of Spirit and the Spirit realms. The Spirit realms and Spirit cannot be seen from the physical because as with water vapour in the air, it is light, intangible and often imperceptible. Spirit can interpenetrate the physical because it is made of finer materials just as air can hold water vapour before the cold slows its vibration down to form water and then ice.

To continue this analogy, for Spirit to communicate with us or for us to communicate with Spirit, each must learn to control their vibrational state. Spirit must be able to slow their vibration so they can be perceived by us while we must learn to speed ours up to be able to hear and see

Spirit. Remember that activities such as meditation, prayerfulness, and quiet contemplation raise our vibrational state.

The lower realms of the Spirit world can be likened more to water. It should be noted that the closer the vibrational states of the lower realms are to the physical, the more grounded those living there are in physicality. As the vibration of Spirit speeds up, it becomes less accessible to those below. This is very true for those in Spirit, for there are many intermediate levels as we move closer to the high vibrational rate of the God Source. I would also note that it is much easier for those above to slow their vibration down to speak to those in the lower realms than for those in the lower realms to raise theirs.

So the Spirit body penetrates and is held within the physical body. The Spirit is not trapped but it is attached for the physical life that the soul has chosen by a silver cord. Upon death this cord is severed. There are many reports of sensitives seeing the separation of the physical body from the Spirit body and the breaking of the silver cord.

In the Bible in Ecclesiastes 12:6 we read,

> *"Remember him before the silver cord is snapped . . . before the dust returns to the earth as it began and the Spirit returns to God who gave it."*

Another proof that we can look to for support of the idea of two bodies and eternal life are "out-of-body experiences" and "near-death experiences." These occur when the physical body is separated from the etheric but the silver cord continues to connect you.

Out-of-body experiences happen more than you might think. Every night while your physical body sleeps, you are able to enter the astral world—the Spirit realms—to learn, explore and visit loved ones. Often we do not remember these excursions. There are many instances where people have found themselves looking down at their sleeping body connected by the silver cord. Sometimes this can be quite frightening, because they do not understand the experience and do not know how they will get back into the body. There is little for them to fear. This is a normal state to be in and it is called astral projection. Once they get over the shock of the experience, they can choose to return easily and comfortably. If they remain in a state of panic, any loud noise or an alarm will snap them back into the body.

A near-death experience is similar in that it is a separation of the Spirit body from the physical body brought on by an illness, an accident or the momentary death of the physical body. The soul which has been thrown from the body believes that it is time to make the transition and begin its journey to the Heaven World only to be stopped and told that it is not time yet. No matter what science tells you, these experiences are real. Science has an important stake in these experiences not being true. If they are true, then it changes the nature of the world scientists understand.

It has been my experience over the last thirty years that many more people have had life changing experiences with those from the Spirit realm than would like to admit it. There is a social stigma associated with these types of experiences and most tend to keep their experiences to themselves rather than have to bear the scrutiny and disbelief of those around them. You who have had such experiences are not alone. The more people who come forward with their stories the more we validate the experiences of others who have not shared theirs.

To Spiritualists and gifted intuitives, there are many proofs affirming the reality of a life after death. We have only explored a few here. Each of us must deal with the death of the physical body in our own way. There is much evidence and for many of us, certain proof, that we are eternal, and that a brighter world of love and light awaits us. We are both the caterpillar and the butterfly.

Appreciate Each Day

Each day is precious unto itself. To fully appreciate each day, you must think of it as the very last time this day will be here to be used and lived in.

No matter how similar the days, this one will never again be repeated. How do you want to spend this last day? In appreciation of its gifts? In excitement of its possibilities?

Spirit Message using Ouiji Board

Spirit Speaks
Messages shared through Spirit-Medium
Rev. Barry King, Ph.D.

The following excerpt is from a "Spirit Channelling Session" on February 27, 2003 with one of our regular groups. (*The process is relatively easy and natural for an experienced medium. It is without dramatics and most often very quiet and gentle. I do not go into a trance but I do achieve an altered state which allows me to step aside and let Spirit work through me. Our sessions are taped and the following is not edited or modified but is written exactly as it was spoken.*)

Guide 1: David George speaking through Barry. This vessel is in a time of transition . . . . There is much to do for we are creating a vehicle through which the message of love, the message of eternal life, the message of responsible action, the message of hope is to be transmitted to an eager people.

We are busy working with many in the physical attempting to create a bridge—a bridge of awareness, a bridge of Light, for there is much Light waiting to be absorbed into the physical world but it is hampered by the negativity, intolerance and impatience of those who will receive. We, however, can assure you that we are patient, we are tolerant, we are forgiving and we know as with any child, it is the first steps which are the most difficult. We are there to hold the hands of our children as they step into a greater awareness, into a higher vibration, into the work which must be done.

There is a plan. There is a cycle. There are some who know and understand this plan and this cycle. They are not heard, for it is not time. The message of Spirit is heard as it can be heard; is understood when it is time to be understood; is translated into action when action is called for. There is a plan. There is order. What appears to be chaos to you is not. Count the days, count the years, for change is in the wind. We will, you will, transform into a more meaningful and purposeful undertaking. There is a plan. We celebrate the journey; we fill the hearts of our children with hope. We take the first steps. The marvel of the plan is that it is unknown and unseen by those who participate in it. Faith, right action, and love are the tools. I am in transition *(meaning that a Higher vibrational entity is entering)*. I bid you farewell.

The Immortality of the Soul

The following is an exploration of the soul as presented by various religious traditions. The soul or Spirit is characterized as the Divine Self in Hinduism, as the product of conditions and causes in Buddhism, as the core of the individual person, and his or her choices and deeds in Judaism, Christianity, and Islam. Buddhism does not conceive of the soul as ultimately real.

The soul, in any of these varied conceptions, is more essential to a person's identity than is his or her body, which is made from clay and is but a vestment, a possession, something one has rather than what one is. From an interfaith perspective, this notion or understanding that we are by nature Spirit reaffirms the belief that no matter what our religion or faith path, we are all brothers and sisters in the eyes of God. The scriptures also discuss how the soul survives the death of the physical body. Although an understanding of the manner of its survival varies among the religions—it may remain close to earth, ascend to Heaven, descend into hell, participate in a general resurrection, merge into the Godhead, or transmigrate into another body—its survival is a common thread that unites all traditions.

> The body is the sheath of the soul. *Judaism. Talmud, Sanhedrin 108a*

> The dust returns to the earth as it was, and the Spirit returns to God who gave it. *Judaism and Christianity. Bible, Ecclesiastes 12.7*

Then the Lord God formed man out of the dust of the ground, and breathed into his nostrils the breath of life; and man became a living being. *Judaism and Christianity. Bible, Genesis 2.7*

And He originated the creation of man out of clay, then He fashioned his progeny of an extraction of mean water, then He shaped him, and breathed His Spirit in him. *Islam. Qur'an 32.8-9*

The union of seed and power produces all things; the escape of the soul brings about change. Through this we come to know the conditions of outgoing and returning spirits. *Confucianism. I Ching, Great Commentary 1.4.2*

Now my breath and Spirit goes to the Immortal, and this body ends in ashes; OM. O Mind! remember. Remember the deeds. Remember the actions. *Hinduism. Isha Upanishad 17, Yajur Veda 40.15*

The outward form, brethren, of him who has won the truth stands before you, but that which binds it to rebirth is cut in twain. *Buddhism. Digha Nikaya, Brahmajala Sutta*

The soul is characterized by knowledge and vision, is formless, is an agent, has the same extent as its own body, is the enjoyer of the fruits of karmas, and exists in samsara. It is also enlightened and has a characteristic upward motion. *Jainism. Nemichandra, Dravyasangraha 2*

Matter has no life, hence it has no real existence. Mind is immortal. *Christian Science. Science and Health, 584*

A man is his own immortal soul. *Scientology. L. Ron Hubbard, A New Slant on Life*

Knowing that this body is like foam, and comprehending that it is as unsubstantial as a mirage, one should destroy the flower-tipped shafts of sensual passions [Mara], and

pass beyond the sight of the King of death. *Buddhism.*
Dhammapada 46

Know that the present life is but a sport and a diversion,
an adornment and a cause of boasting among you, and a
rivalry in wealth and children. It is as a rain whose vegetation
pleases the unbelievers; then it withers, and you see it turning
yellow, then it becomes straw. And in the Hereafter there is
grievous punishment, and forgiveness from God and good
pleasure; whereas the present life is but the joy of delusion.
Islam. Qur'an 57.20

Man's real nature is primarily spiritual life, which weaves
its threads of mind to build a cocoon of flesh, encloses its
own soul in the cocoon, and, for the first time, the Spirit
becomes flesh. Understand this clearly: The cocoon is not
the silkworm; In the same way, the physical body is not
man but merely man's cocoon. Just as the silkworm will
break out of its cocoon and fly free, so, too, will man break
out of his body-cocoon and ascend to the spiritual world
when his time is come. Never think that the death of the
physical body is the death of man. Since man is life, he will
never know death. *Seicho-no-ie. Nectarean Shower of Holy*
Doctrines. (Dhammapada 46: Cf. Sutra of Hui Neng 10,
p. 437. Qur'an 57.20: Cf. Qur'an 17.18-19, p. 336; 102,
p. 340. Nectarean Shower of Holy Doctrines: As in popular
Japanese Buddhism, the scripture of this new religion contrasts
the realm of appearances and sense impressions with the realm
of Reality. The body belongs to the realm of appearances, but
the spiritual life belongs to the order of Reality.)

You prefer this life, although the life to come is better and
more enduring. All this is written in earlier scriptures; the
scriptures of Abraham and Moses. *Islam. Qur'an 87.16-19*

Onyame does not die, I will therefore not die. African
Traditional Religions. *Akan Proverb (Ghana) (Akan Proverb:*

'Onyame' is the most common Akan name for the Supreme Being. It means, roughly 'the One who gives fullness.')

Do not say, "They are dead!" about anyone who is killed for God's sake. Rather they are living, even though you do not notice it. *Islam. Qur'an 2.154*

One who identifies himself with his soul regards bodily transmigration of his soul at death fearlessly, like changing one cloth for another. *Jainism. Pujyapada, Samadhishataka 77*

Some day the Great Chief Above will overturn the mountains and the rocks. Then the Spirits that once lived in the bones buried there will go back into them. At present, those Spirits live in the tops of the mountains, watching their children on earth and waiting for the great change which is to come. The voices of these Spirits can be heard in the mountains at all times. Mourners who wail for their dead hear Spirit voices reply, and thus they know that their lost ones are always near. *Native American Religions. Yakima Tradition*

Birth is not a beginning; death is not an end. There is existence without limitation; there is continuity without a starting point. Existence without limitation is space. Continuity without a starting point is time. There is birth, there is death, there is issuing forth, there is entering in. That through which one passes in and out without seeing its form, that is the Portal of God. *Taoism. Chuang Tzu 23*

But someone will ask, "How are the dead raised? With what kind of body do they come?" You foolish man! What you sow does not come to life unless it dies. And what you sow is not the body which is to be, but a bare kernel, perhaps of wheat or some other grain. But God gives it a body as He has chosen, and to each kind of seed its own body. For not all flesh is alike, but there is one kind for men, another for animals, another for birds, and another for fish. There are celestial bodies and there are terrestrial bodies; but the glory of the celestial is one, and the glory of the terrestrial is another. There is one glory of the sun, and another glory of the moon, and another glory of the stars; for star differs from star in glory. So it is with the resurrection from the dead. What is sown is perishable, what is raised is imperishable. It is sown in dishonour, it is raised in glory. It is sown in weakness, it is raised in power. It is sown in a physical body, it is raised in a spiritual body. If there is a physical body, there is also a spiritual body. *Christianity. Bible, 1 Corinthians 15.35-44*

All humanity born into the land of sun-origin, this Land of Japan, Come from the kami, And to the kami will return. *Shinto. Naokata Nakanishi, One Hundred Poems on The Way of Death*

As you can see, the immortality of the soul is a central belief held by most, if not all traditions. It would appear to me, that how the soul is understood is a reflection of not only the religious tradition but also the culture and the times that it grew from.

As someone who works with Spirit every day, I have been blessed to have seen, communicated and worked with those in the Spirit Realms. I have had the opportunity to have glimpses of the Heaven World and the life that awaits us all. Yet even though the truth of our immortality is affirmed in the writings of religious traditions and validated by experiences with those in the Heaven World, many still reject its reality and are fearful. Over the years, one of the greatest gifts that I have been able to share with people is the certain knowledge that we are eternal and that there is no death.

Embracing an Infinite God

Winter in Atlantic Canada can be long and cold. One of the things that makes the winter easier to cope with is the certainty that the spring will follow. In no time at all, spring will arrive with all of its colour and beauty and vigour. We know this even though the world outside is dark and cold. Spring and the renewal of the world around us is a certainty. We can count on it.

Sometimes it is good to have a reminder that there is order in the universe, and that the chaos that we seem to be experiencing is not chaos at all. The chaos is an illusion not because the confusion or uncertainty we are experiencing is not real, but because we cannot see the big picture. We do not have all the facts and, therefore, we lack the perspective to make a real judgement of the true state of things. We need to be reminded that just because we do not see the order of things does not mean that it has no order or that it does not make sense.

From its beginnings, the history of humanity has been largely a search for understanding—a search for order in what appeared to be a chaotic universe. We now have an understanding of many natural laws and this understanding is evolving and changing at an alarming rate. We have learned a great deal and now can explore the heavens searching for greater understanding. We should not and cannot, however, let ourselves become satisfied or complacent with our great understanding. We have only touched the edge of eternity. In 1928, the Registrar of Patents in the United States tendered his resignation, stating that his function was no longer valid because everything that could be invented had by that day received a patent. In an infinite universe, with infinite possibilities, created by an infinite and incomprehensible God we can never have total understanding or awareness. This is exciting to me because it means I have a lifetime of discovery ahead of me and that each discovery will open new mysteries to be explored. It is humbling because no matter what I understand, there will always be more. Humbling because I realize that I can only understand things from the narrow perspective of an entity immersed in a physical life on a planet called Earth somewhere in the universe.

When we start thinking about different traditions or approaches to spiritual life, it is important to realize that our understanding will always be imperfect. It is not because God is imperfect; it is because God is infinite and incomprehensible. We, with our limited perspective, can only have a small understanding of something which is infinite. We cannot even begin to embrace an understanding of timelessness, of dimensionality, or of the infinite. God is infinite and by this mere fact, God is diversity. How can we believe that there can be only one right path to the infinite? What an injustice this is to attempt to shackle humanity to a limited understanding while speaking of the infinite. By definition, the infinite is diversity.

Life is full of uncertainty and it is that uncertainty which provides the opportunity to make choices. We feel that we are surrounded by uncertainty but in truth there is order. From every challenge, we are given the chance to grow, to learn, to become. There are no absolutes in an infinite universe and things are, on the large scale, not predictable. We have to trust our process. We have to know that we are moving along the path to our own best good. That does not always mean that it is the easy path. Sometimes it is very hard, but it is important to understand that it is purposeful. That life provides us with opportunity and that we have been blessed with the gift of free will.

Images like this from the Hubble Telescope give us a sense of scale when we are talking about an infinite universe. Here you are looking at a deep space view of not stars but galaxies. Image Courtesy of Nasa.

I believe that "faith" is not about believing that everything will be looked after for you if you embrace the one true understanding of God. I believe that "faith" is knowing that life is purposeful and we can trust our process to get us where we need to be, to learn or experience what we need to achieve—that greater plan that we cannot know. If we could see the great plan—our Divine Plan, our opportunity for choice would be removed. God loves us and provides us with the challenges and opportunities we need to achieve that which is for our own best good. We are learning and growing and becoming.

This spring, as the world around you experiences its rebirth, celebrate life and experience your own renewal. Embrace the awareness that life is purposeful and that we are blessed with infinite possibilities. Have faith that you have what you need in life to be happy and that the world is unfolding as it should. Know that you are loved and that there is no need to get caught up in the chaos of the physical. Know that you have the tools which you need to meet the challenges that you have chosen. You are part of the order which surrounds you and just as spring always follows winter, you can count on the fact that you will find happiness and joy.

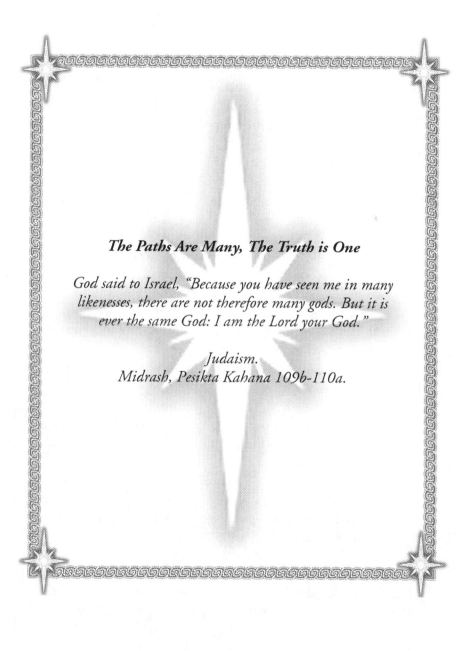

The Paths Are Many, The Truth is One

God said to Israel, "Because you have seen me in many likenesses, there are not therefore many gods. But it is ever the same God: I am the Lord your God."

Judaism.
Midrash, Pesikta Kahana 109b-110a.

Each Day is a Gift!

Are you caught up in the hustle and bustle of modern life? Do you wake up each day and wonder how you will get through it? Would you like to wake up each morning and wonder with joy what challenges life will offer you today?

There is a simple starting point to getting rid of all the unproductive thoughts you have at the beginning of, and during, each day. That starting point is recognizing the fact that each day is a gift.

Recognize that when you came into this life, you were allotted a life's worth of time—a lifetime—to be used encased in your physical body. Recognize that each day is precious unto itself. To fully appreciate each day, you must think of it as the very last time this day will be here to be used and lived in. No matter how similar the days, this one will never again be repeated. This means that every moment of every day is precious. Every moment is unique.

In the physical, we can learn to live each moment to its fullest. We are eternal but this does not mean we should take our existence, our consciousness for granted. It does not mean that we should not celebrate each moment of awareness as the precious gift that it is. Look around you. You are aware and conscious. You are alive. What a wondrous thing! What a joyous thing to be part of the dance of life.

It is only here in the physical that we can feel the press of time. It is only in the physical that we can feel that time is limited. Use this awareness to cultivate a joy in each moment, in each challenge, and in each failure and success. You are learning and growing. Learn to live in the moment. Learn to reap the bounty from your existence.

Rev Barry King

Embracing Diversity:
The Challenge of the 21ˢᵗ Century

Since September 11ᵗʰ, 2001, we have seen the impact of intolerance and fear of things that are different. We have seen the twin towers fall and renewed fighting in the Middle East. We have seen loving people, held hostage by fear, respond through intolerance and prejudice. The responses can be extreme as exhibited by terrorists or more subtle such as when we quietly resist positive change or refuse to acknowledge the right of others to be different. It seems to me that one of the greatest challenges we of the 21ˢᵗ Century must face is embracing without fear the diversity which surrounds us.

A hundred years ago, each of us probably would have lived in a small geographical area for most of our lives. We would have had very little exposure to other cultures, other peoples or other ways. In fact, we would have probably been afraid of things that we did not understand or that were new and alien to us. Like many people of the time, we may have retreated to that which was familiar for safety and security. Over thousands of years, human nature has caused us to reject that which we did not understand.

We lived in a small world. We rejected change and retreated to what we knew. We can no longer live in the security of a small world. The world has changed. We are the children of a new world and to live in it we must embrace new ways. I think we live in wondrous times. Unlike a hundred years ago, today we are connected to a global community—we are connected to the world. Unlike any other time in human history, we are blessed with the opportunity to experience the landscape, the cultures and the peoples of the world in ways that have never been possible before. We have gone beyond the limitations of mother earth and have seen the birth of stars and walked on other celestial bodies

Yet we live in fear because we cannot let go of our small world ways. We do not understand that even though the world is filled with many cultures and many ways, we are one people. We still retreat from that which is different and fear that which we do not understand. Even though the world has changed, and we see its myriad of forms and peoples, we have been afraid to embrace our new heritage—to free ourselves with a clearer view of the truth.

In a complex world, accepting diversity allows us to experience a richer and more beautiful world. When we look at the beautiful, diverse world that God has created for us to live in, it is clear to us that God is a God of diversity. There is not just one type of tree, or one type of bird, or one type of flower, or one type of person. The world is populated with a multitude of forms which are trees, and birds, and flowers, and people in all shapes, sizes and colour. This diversity makes the world more beautiful.

If we believe that God is infinite and incomprehensible, then one place to begin to understand God is to embrace the knowledge that in this diverse and beautiful world created by God, it is only natural that God should manifest the message of unconditional love in many ways to many peoples. God is a God of many faces. We in the Interfaith Ministry celebrate these many faces of God represented by different religious traditions and rejoice that we have been given such a beautiful and diverse world. We express this truth with the phrase, "*The paths are many, the truth is one. Love thy neighbour.*"

Today there are many types of spiritual healers. Some call what they do therapeutic touch, some call it laying-on-of-hands, some are Reiki Healers, or do Touch for Life, some are energy workers, or channel the healing energy of angels. All are working with the same energy—attuning to the same vibrations. Some new names arise from a person's discovery of something that was unknown to them and, therefore, they do not know that it is also known by another name. Some new names come from the perceived need to make a thing more acceptable or understood. Some new names are an attempt to own it or control it or to make it their own. Even though they are utilizing fundamentally the same energy, there is the potential for each type of practitioner to see themselves as better than the others, as separate and distinct, possessing an exclusive truth and not part of a greater community—the community of people who work with healing energies. I am not picking on the energy healers for most of them do not see their gift as separate from the rest. However, it is important to see how this lack of information and understanding can manifest itself and separate people.

There are those who want to own God and to control how we understand God. The Interfaith Ministry believes that we cannot own God because God is infinite and incomprehensible. An infinite God cannot be encapsulated within a restrictive doctrine. Spiritual healing is spiritual healing no matter what you call it. Love is love no matter what type of box you put it in. Good people are good people no matter how they choose to worship or celebrate God. Good and loving people will stand together in the Heaven World no matter what tradition they embraced in the physical world. We, in the Interfaith Ministry, are committed to helping people develop their awareness of other people and of other ways. We reject the notion that there is only one right way.

The other day, I was talking to someone when it became apparent to me that we were both saying the same thing even though we did not know it. We were using the words that we had learned within our understanding to say basically the same thing even though we felt we were in conflict. Sometimes language can be a terrible barrier and can separate us.

In the Bible, Genesis 11, Chapters 1-9 we read about the tower of Babel:

> *Now the whole world had one language and a common speech.*
> *As men moved eastward, they found a plain in Shinar and*

settled there. They said to each other, "Come, let's make bricks and bake them thoroughly." They used brick instead of stone, and tar for mortar. Then they said, "Come, let us build ourselves a city, with a tower that reaches to the heavens, so that we may make a name for ourselves and not be scattered over the face of the whole earth."

But the LORD came down to see the city and the tower that the men were building. The LORD said, "If as one people speaking the same language they have begun to do this, then nothing they plan to do will be impossible for them. Come, let us go down and confuse their language so they will not understand each other."

So the LORD scattered them from there over all the earth and they stopped building the city. That is why it was called Babel—because there the LORD confused the language of the whole world. From there the LORD scattered them over the face of the whole earth.

There are many kinds of language and many ways that we understand it. There are spoken languages but within them there are other forms of language which are not so apparent. Sometimes a gesture or a look can speak more than any words. This hidden or perceptual language can join or separate us. We can speak through fear or love. We can speak through joy or despair. We can celebrate each other's successes or choose not to. Sometimes it is not the words that people hear but the emotions or the misconceptions. If I say the words Priest, Rabbi, Monk, Holy Man, Witch Doctor, Priestess, High Priest, Minister, Yogi or Shaman to you, what perception or emotion or feeling is connected to each of these words? All are servants of God, ministering to their people and should all be seen or understood in the same light. We should have a positive feeling for all of them. Do we or does the language of misconception, or prejudice or ignorance get in the way?

We can connect emotions and feelings to words and may even speak the words with emotions which are perceived by the listener. This can change the meaning of the word. To embrace diversity, as the children of the New World, we must reject our limitations of language and learn to speak one language, the language of love and compassion. The language that is of Spirit and not grounded in negativity and fear—a language of truth.

Within diversity, we are often saying the same thing but are separated by the fact that we are using a different language and do not choose to understand each other. As one people embracing diverse perspectives of God and God's love, we can change the world. We believe that the world we live in is a reflection of our thoughts. Language plays an important role in our thoughts. We can embrace diversity and learn to speak one language. As in the story of Babel, we need to be as one people. If we can overcome the restrictions of language and embrace a greater truth we will be able to do anything. We will be able to change the world from a small dark place of fear and intolerance into a place where an infinite God can manifest through each of us a message of love and light.

The God I know and understand is a God of unconditional love. God does not persecute those of the Light who shine blue or green instead of white. We are all aspects of the one Light and truth. Loving people, whatever their faith, will stand together in the world of Spirit. There, as here, they will have reason to celebrate. We have been given a beautiful, wondrous and diverse world. We have been given the opportunity to exercise our free will to learn and grow. We have been given the opportunity to love. We have been given a beautiful and diverse world to live in. Celebrate it with each breath!

In closing, I say to you, support those servants of the Light who walk along a different path. Support those who have a different path but serve the God of their understanding and bring love and joy into the world. How will you recognize them? They will know that they are not perfect and that they are not in possession of an exclusive truth. They will work through love and not fear or hate. They will seek and not reject truths which force them to re-examine their understanding of the world. Truth seekers from all faiths, who reject fear, are your brothers and sisters. They rejoice in the knowledge that others have found God's Light through another path. Diversity makes us richer and our understanding more complete.

From this day on, try to look at the world with eyes of wonder and celebrate the diversity in your life. Make a commitment to peace. We must do more than be tolerant of different ways, we must celebrate the opportunities they provide for us to grow and to experience a richer and more beautiful world. Rejoice in the knowledge that the joy and love in your heart is of the Light and that one day you will stand with your brothers and sisters from all faiths together in the world of Spirit.

The Paths are Many, the Truth is One

When appearances and names are put away and all discrimination ceases, that which remains is the true and essential nature of things and, as nothing can be predicated as to the nature of essence, is called the "Suchness" of Reality. This universal, undifferentiated, inscrutable Suchness is the only Reality, but it is variously characterized as Truth, Mind-essence, Transcendental Intelligence, Perfection of Wisdom, etc. This Dharma of the imagelessness of the Essence-nature of Ultimate Reality is the Dharma which has been proclaimed by all the Buddhas, and when all things are understood in full agreement with it, one is in possession of Perfect Knowledge.

Buddhism.
Lankavatara Sutra

P. John Burden

The Cold Within

It is now the year 2009 and we have been waging a war against terrorist for almost a decade. Today I was listening to the radio and it appears that it's a war that cannot be won. It occurred to me that the enemy is not terrorism at all. The real enemy will never be defeated with violence and war. The real enemy is fear and intolerance. The real enemy is hatred and prejudice. The real enemy is born out of war, not conquered by war. The real enemy is born out of ignorance.

We must look at how we face the challenges that events like September 11, 2001 teach us. Has history taught us so little or is it that we choose not to understand? While thinking about this, I was reminded of a poem that I had read once.

The Cold Within

Six humans trapped by happenstance
In a dark and bitter cold,
Each one possessed a stick of wood
Or so the story's told.

Their dying fire in need of logs
The first woman held hers back,
For on the faces around the fire
She noticed one was black.

The next man looking cross the way
Saw one not of his church,

And couldn't bring himself to give
The fire his stick of birch.

The third one sat in tattered clothes
He gave his coat a hitch,
Why should his log be put to use
To warm the idle rich?

The rich man just sat back and thought
Of the wealth he had in store,
And how to keep what he had earned
From the lazy, shiftless poor.

The black man's face bespoke revenge
As the fire passed from sight,
For all he saw in the stick of wood
Was a chance to spite the white.

The last man in this forlorn group
Did naught except for gain,
Giving to only those who filled his purse
Was how he played the game.

The logs held tight in death's still hands
Was proof of human sin,
They didn't die from the cold without
They died from—THE COLD WITHIN.

Author Unknown

How many of us do not know this cold? Few of us have not felt its harsh and unforgiving bite. Few of us have not, at some time, felt its chill freeze our hearts. This cold is insidious for not only does it cause people to suffer injustice, hate, and intolerance but it can also breed those very qualities in its victims. It feeds on itself causing us to react and behave in ways that we most dislike in others.

The phrase *"Do unto others as you would have them do unto you"* warns us of this tendency. We all have work to do. There is much that we can learn! Each of us is on a path of tests and trials and challenges. It is important to understand that we are all where we should be to learn what we must learn. It is also true that even though we are all different, there is much that we share in common.

How many of you have suffered because you were perceived to be different? Because you do not believe what others believe? It has always amazed me that so many people fear those who see the world differently than they do. In some strange quirk of perception, it appears that people who all think the same can feel special by deciding that everyone else, who does not think the way they do, is crazy or lesser or evil or dangerous. Terrorists manifest the extremes of fear and intolerance. If we think about it, a lesser form of terrorism is occurring in our streets and playgrounds every day. How do we deal with it? It is important however, that we think very carefully about how we address the problem. In a climate of hatred and fear when one terrorist falls, two more rise up.

One of the problems is the tendency of one person to judge another not necessarily through awareness but through ignorance. Judgement of others is futile. It is usually how we avoid looking at ourselves. History has shown that eventually those who judge are judged. Just because we choose to believe that everyone else is wrong, does not by default make us right.

In a loving world, it is our differences that make each of us special. The price for this is that it can be hard to place yourself above everyone else if you accept that we all are special. Learn about other ways and other peoples and come to know their specialness—their uniqueness. We tend to fear what we do not understand.

There are names for the cold within. One name is prejudice. Another is intolerance. Some call it, unjust. No matter what we call this cold, it is wrong. It divides and separates people. It kills the mind and limits the soul. It allows people to look at others as lesser souls than themselves. It is a darkness that hides the Light. It is the only real enemy and it can be beaten.

A hundred years ago, people's intelligence and their potential in society was judged by examining the shape of the head. People who had the wrong shaped head were thought to be useless and lazy. It was thought they couldn't learn. These people with the wrong shaped heads could not get jobs and were not encouraged to get an education. Throughout history, as today, there have been many false indicators of worth and potential used. These include sex, colour, race, weight, height, social class, religion, colour of hair, length of hair, distance between the eyes, where you live and many, many more. Look around you today and see if you can see how people try to measure people. Reject them all—all of them feed the cold.

We are all brothers and sisters in Spirit, no matter what place we hold in the physical. Choose the path which rejects intolerance and prejudice. I do not need to tell you that intolerance and prejudice does not come from love and truth, or that prejudice embraces qualities which are not spiritual and reflect the lower vibrations found in the physical such as anger, hate, fear, envy, lust, and greed. The cold within exists only in the absence of love.

How do we defeat the enemy? Rejoice in our differences. Embrace the truth that there are many ways to love and that each path has a special character. People of all cultures and traditions can and do love. These people are of the Light and the Light is of God. Together, as loving souls, we will learn to overcome the enemy. We will not only survive the cold without but we will also not die from the cold that comes from within.

The Mismeasure of People

About thirty years ago, I read a book called <u>The Mismeasure of Man</u> by Harvard palaeontologist, Stephen Jay Gould. It was a fascinating and, actually, a disturbing book which explored the many measures that society (people) have chosen to use to judge people over the centuries. It discussed the flawed work of scientists and religious leaders who struggled to validate the measures they were using to place whole groups of people into categories for judgement. Some of the complicated measures used included facial features, distance between the eyes, bumps on the head, colour of the skin or hair, place of birth, etc. You get the picture. These measures were fabricated and given validation to help people feel comfortable with their prejudice and intolerance to differences. There had to be conformity and people had to work within their own social strata. To deviate from this accepted view would destroy society and create chaos or so it was believed.

These "mismeasures" were grounded in people's fears of the unknown or their need to be better than some other group of people. One of the most obvious measures was race and scientists grounded in the need to validate their perspective could "scientifically" prove that there were greater and lesser races. Their race, of course, being the greater race.

These "mismeasures" were also reinforced by religious leaders who reflected back to the people the prejudice and intolerance generated. They also placed a new layer of fear and separation on the people. Not only were there greater and lesser races but there were also greater and lesser ways to understand God. Those lesser races and lesser people were never going to make it to Heaven and would burn in eternal hellfire.

The most disturbing point about the book is not that these "mismeasures" happened, but tragically that they are still happening and that some of the same "mismeasures" are being used today to reinforce prejudice and intolerance. Sadly people are still reacting from the fear of what they do not understand and looking for a world where there are no differences. Most disturbing of all is the fact that in a world which has information readily accessible about other peoples and ways, that we still chose to live in ignorance. I know a loving couple who have been together for many years. This couple suffers daily from one of the "mismeasures" that people use to judge people. This couple is afraid to be seen together as a couple. They are afraid of what the neighbours will think and how they will react to them. They are afraid to tell their families and worry about the stigma if their secret was to be found out. They live in fear, because they love each other. They are good people. They are loving people. They are your neighbours, your brothers, yours sisters, your friends, your daughters and your sons.

This couple I am describing 40 years ago may have been a Protestant and a Catholic. This couple 30 years ago may have been a black and a white couple or from two different races or nationalities. This couple 15 years ago may have been multi-faith from two different traditions. This couple five years ago may have had 20 years difference in age between them. Today this couple is a same-sex couple who wish to celebrate their love for each other in a free and loving society.

Recently there has been much talk in the media about same-sex couples and same-sex marriages. I have heard many "mismeasures" used to validate the prejudice and intolerance some people feel. I have heard it said that "if same-sex marriages are legalized, it will destroy the social fabric and bring about the destruction of the family." Loving people, no matter what race, shape, size, colour, religion, or sexual orientation will never be responsible for the destruction of what is good about our social fabric and families. We can only hope that they will be responsible for the destruction of what is NOT good, and NOT loving.

In Spirit, we are not male or female. Those researching reincarnation tell us that in some lives we chose to be male, and in others we chose to be female. Given this and the great deal of evidence from Spirit that we are all God's children and are here in this life to learn and grow, it seems incongruent to suggest that either a homosexual or a heterosexual lifestyle will get us into the Heaven world. It is more likely that no matter what orientation you have, it is whether or not you are a loving and kind person (or couple) that will open Heaven's gates to you.

One of the things we may never be able to measure is the suffering and pain that has been caused by people judging other people through ignorance and fear. Let us all do our part in creating a loving world that will have no place for such "mismeasures" and that in time such thinking will be only a dim memory of a barbaric past.

You are Changing the World

I turned on the news last night. People are still fighting wars and violent crimes are up. Intolerance and greed can still be seen in countries all over the world. The environment is still under siege. Extinctions are rising and soil erosion is becoming a global concern. The ozone layer which protects all living things from harmful ultraviolet rays is still being destroyed. After over twenty years of intense attention, we are no farther ahead with the battle against pollution. More and more people are suffering from depression, and suicides are increasing as people feel more hopeless. The news was not encouraging.

I believe, however, if we look past the events of the day, there is a bigger picture we can see from watching the news. For a moment, let us look at the source of many of the problems facing the world today. Let's see? We have war, pollution, ozone depletion, soil erosion, loneliness, depression. It would appear that the central player in all of these concerns is "people." It is striking to realize the power that "these people" have on the state of the world that we live in. Let us make the word "people" a little less impersonal. Let us give these people a name. Who are these people? Well, I guess the answer to that is simple. *WE ARE THE PEOPLE!*

Ask yourself, how many times this week have I been impatient? How many times have I been intolerant or unkind? Have I reached out to help others or only to help myself? How much have I done for the environment? Do I bother to buy environmentally friendly products or do I go for convenience and low price? Do I take responsibility for my actions or do I blame consequences on an unseen force?

Spirit tells us that "thoughts are things" and that "each thought is a prayer." We—you—are changing the world! If the news of the future is to reflect a more positive picture, then we must accept responsibility for our actions. Reflect is the right word because the state of things in your world is a direct consequence of the type of thoughts that you harbour. If your thoughts fill you with pettiness and fear, then the world you live in will reflect this. If they fill you with joy and love, then the world you live in will reflect this. Which world would you like to live in? A world of cynicism or a world of joy!

You are changing the world. Many of us will look at the big picture and feel powerless. We forget that the big picture is made up of many small parts. Changing the world is changing ourselves, and it does not happen all at once. It takes time.

Here is a story about a research project I read about a number of years ago. I would like to share it with you.

A researcher was studying a group of rhesus monkeys on a chain of small islands. He noted that one of the main foods of these monkeys was potatoes. He found that on one of these remote Islands, one monkey, one day took its potato to the riverside and began to wash it. He noted this with interest because it was the first time he had seen this happen. Within a few weeks, he discovered that many of the monkeys on this island had learned to wash their potatoes too. He assumed that they had seen the first monkey and had learned the behaviour. This was probably true for the monkeys on the first Island. It was a learned behaviour.

However, all of a sudden, the researcher was seeing monkeys on other Islands washing their potatoes too. Within a few months, all the monkeys on all the islands were washing their potatoes. How did he explain this?

He called it the 100ʰ monkey theory. This theory was that at a certain point (the 100ʰ monkey) the behaviour of washing potatoes had become part of the consciousness of all the monkeys simultaneously. That is the behaviour had reached a critical mass and once it did all the monkeys on all the Islands developed the desire to wash their potatoes before eating them.

I have noted similar happenings in my life in the world around me. It is that critical mass that we are looking for. All you can do, however, is do the best that you can do. If we all do the best that we can, eventually we will reach the critical mass we need for people's consciousness to change and become more positive. If you embrace love, compassion, kindness, you will make the world—your world—a better place.

One of the lessons that we have to learn, however, is that we should not judge others. We do not know the path that others are travelling nor do we know the lessons they must learn. Try not to judge. Be tolerant of other ways and recognize that the only person you can take responsibility for is you. That is often hard enough. Sometimes judging others is how we avoid looking at ourselves.

You have all heard about affirmations. You can program yourself to be more positive if you use them just as you can program yourself to be more negative by using negative affirmations. An example of a negative affirmation is when you are given a task and you tell yourself that you cannot do it. You might say, "I can't do this because I am too tired, or too inexperienced, or too stressed, or too important, too clumsy, etc." Be assured that, if you believe that you cannot do it, *you will not do it!*

A positive affirmation is just the opposite and works best when stated as an event that has reached a positive conclusion. If you are quitting smoking, your affirmation might be "I do not smoke" or "I give thanks for being a non-smoker." When you go to bed at night instead of thinking about all that went wrong during the day, you should do an inventory of all the positive things that happened during the day and give thanks for the challenges that you faced. Affirmations can be used effectively to change your behaviour and your thought patterns.

Contrary to all that you may have been taught, it is not your actions that change the world. It is your thoughts. Thoughts that are translated—manifested through action. There are no kind or compassionate acts without kind or compassionate thoughts. We have all seen the emptiness of action where there is no thought or intention.

You are here on this planet in this lifetime to change the world. You are an agent of change. You are who you are for a reason. Each star has a place in the universe, just as each of us has a place in the cycle of growth and life on this planet.

Someday the news on the television will be full of wonderful accomplishments and joy. We will have changed the world. Choose the future—now!

On Angel's Wings
Transformational Encounters with Spirit!

Healing Angel

I would like to share with you an experience I had about twenty-five years ago. I have been sensitive to Spirit all my life so experiences with those who were in the Spirit world had confirmed to me the reality of a greater life and the survival of the soul after death. I had, however, always tried to avoid such experiences because they made me different and I was not really sure how it all worked.

Sandi and I had been invited to a lecture and demonstration by the gifted spiritual healer, Sharon Forrester. During the lecture, I noticed a Spirit unlike any I had seen before. It was the golden figure of a woman about 5 feet high floating about a foot off the ground. I could see her facial features, her delicate hands and a flowing gown which glowed with the most beautiful light. What made her truly special was the billowing energy which moved at her back and which looked as it billowed in and out not unlike wings. This entity was clearly different than any I had seen before and was I believe a healing angel working with Sharon Forrester. This struck me because up to this point experience had suggested to me that angels were ministering souls who had chosen a path of service and did not look any different than disembodied Spirits. But here was a real angel, separate and distinct from other types of entities that I had seen.

The angel stood beside the healer. As Sharon talked the angel would move out into the audience and touch people. I closed my eyes and opened them again to make sure I wasn't imagining things. I asked those around me if they could see anything. They could not. The angel moved past me several times to touch people looking at me as she passed. I watched this for over a half an hour before Sharon began doing a healing on a volunteer.

Watching the healing was very confirmational for me. The angel's actions were quite unlike anything I would have expected. When Sharon began the healing, the angel stepped into Sharon. I could see the angel's hands and arms superimposed over the healer's with the billowed energy (wings) being clearly seen at the back of the healer. Unexpectedly when Sharon moved her hands to the waist of the person receiving the healing, the angel crouched. Even though Sharon remained standing, I could see the image of the crouched angel superimposed over her and from Sharon's waist came the angel's hands and arms to meet Sharon's hands.

After the workshop, I shared what I had seen with Sharon who was aware that a healing angel worked with her. Like most people, except for sharing it with my wife Sandi, I kept the experience to myself. A few weeks later, I was at another workshop and met a man who had been at Sharon's Healing Workshop. He described to me an angel he had seen. In every detail, it was the angel that I had witness.

For me this experience changed my life. It confirmed for me the power and presence of God in our lives. It proved to me that angels do exist, that they are distinct and that they can heal. It helped set me on a path of service to share with others the message that we are all eternal and that God moves in our lives no matter what faith we are.

Rev Barry King

As You Think, So It Is!

Even through you are surrounded by a physical world, the world that you live in is a world of thoughts. Once you embrace the fact that it is your thoughts that shape the world that you live in, it is easy to see how they can have so much power over your life. It is also much easier to take back control of your life when you accept the basic truth that you *ARE* what you *THINK*.

It is important that we understand that our thoughts are far more concrete than we give them credit for. This means that if we give a thought enough energy it will become manifest. Another way of saying this is "as you think so it is." If you believe the world is an unfriendly place, it will be. If you believe the world is full of joy, you will find joy at every turn.

Thoughts are the foundation of our reality. When our reality is shaken it is because our thoughts are shaken. The world within does not correspond to the world without. This causes confusion and uncertainty.

Many of us spend a great deal of energy trying to calm the storm, the chaos that surrounds us. We focus on all the things out there that have to be fixed—relationships, finances, work, etc. One of the things that we forget or maybe try to avoid is the fact that it is often the storm within that causes us the most distress. It is also the one which we can take the greatest responsibility for. It is this storm which only we can still when it rages out of control.

Have you ever noticed that when you are troubled you are most sensitive to and affected by those things that are happening around you. We are most likely to be impatient, angry, unhappy, irritable when we are feeling unsettled. It is not the world around you that you should be trying to control and shape, it is the world within.

One of the things that often feeds the storm within is fear. It is not what has happened that causes the most worry but what might happen or could happen. We spend hours fearing and worrying about things that are not real. They have no reality except in our thoughts. They could happen and yet rather than take what action we can to best ensure that they don't happen, we worry. We rob ourselves of our strength when we need it the most. We fill ourselves with self-doubt and we take away our joy. Fear is the mind killer. It is fear that can take away your clarity—your balance—your potential.

To reject fear there is a simple rule—do what you can and then let go. React only when there is clarity and try not to spend your time dealing with imaginings. Try not to give things that have not happened presence in your thoughts because to worry about something is to give it strength. Worry gives it power. Worrying gives the thing you fear reality and increases the possibility of it manifesting in the physical world—the world without.

Remember that we measure ourselves not by our deeds but by our thoughts. Doing something out of fear of what will happen if you do not do it, gains you nothing. It becomes a lie and fills you with self-doubt and insecurity. Whatever you do, must be done because you feel it is right not from fear of the consequences if you do not do it.

Also remember that every thought is a prayer. God hears your thoughts whether you call it a prayer or not. As mentioned earlier, treat every thought as if it will become a reality. That means that when you have a negative thought you must learn to transform it into a positive. Affirm that every day is a wonderful, glorious day to be alive. Give thanks for the challenges you have been given to grow and become all you can be. Affirmations are important because they work.

So to change the world you live in, you must change your thoughts. Most people fail, not because they lack ability but because they did not believe they will succeed. Reprogram your mind. Expect good things to happen. See the positive in life's challenges and understand that they are not burdens.

It is helpful to remember that too much time goes in trying to find happiness outside of ourselves. Sometimes we forget that it is how we use our time that can bring us happiness. Each day do what makes you happy and do what you can do to make someone else happy. These are two simple rules that can be very difficult to follow. Sometimes we get so used to being unhappy and stressed that we do not feel normal unless we are unhappy and stressed out. That can make us follow a path to our own unhappiness. But ask yourself, why do I want to be unhappy? Why do I continue to follow a path which robs me of joy?

Each day is a blessing. Make sure that when you make someone else happy, that it is a genuine act of love. When you do this, you make each day a blessing not only for yourself but for someone else too. This will help you find peace.

Each of us should use every moment to grow and meet the challenges we have set for ourselves in this life. This can only be done by living each moment consciously. Allow each moment to unfold into the next with anticipation—with awareness.

Where will I start? There is a simple starting point to getting rid of all the unproductive thoughts you have at the beginning and during each day. That starting point is recognizing the fact that each day is a gift. It is the recognition that when we came into this life, each of us was allotted a life's worth of time (a lifetime) to be used by us encased in our physical body. That means that every moment is precious. Every moment is unique. Recognize that each day is precious unto itself. To fully appreciate each day, you must think of it as the very last time this day will be here to be used and lived in. No matter how similar the days, this one will never again be repeated.

The next step is to transform your thoughts. When you find a negative thought seeping in—transform it to a positive. Accept all things as challenges not burdens. They are opportunities. Accept that all you can do is your best. Once you have done that you have met your responsibility. Learn to let go.

Accept that the world you live in is a world of thought and let your imagination be a vehicle for creativity and problem solving. Know that brute strength seldom has a lasting impact.

Know that you are one of God's Children and that life is purposeful. Celebrate each breath. And finally, Love yourself.

Listening

A century ago news in a letter for a family member in England could take months to get to its destination. Over the last fifty years, the world has become a much smaller place where a message can travel around the world in seconds. We can speak to one another almost instantaneously no matter where we are. We have access to telephones, cell phones, radio, email, satellite, video, digital cable and more. People can speak to the entire world through media like television, and the internet. Today, we have an incredible capacity to communicate with one another.

With all these opportunities to communicate with clarity, one would have hoped that it would translate into an increase in understanding, cooperation, compassion and love among the people of the world. This does not seem to have been the case. When I watch any one of the two hundred television stations to which I have access, I see that the world is still full of strife, that violence in many places is at an all time high, that prejudice is still alive and well, and that there is a lack of communication.

The question we have to ask is: With all these ways to communicate why is there so little understanding? What is the problem? It is true that the world today is a noisy place. Not only are there loud noises which assail our ears but there are many noises which assault our minds—noises that make it very difficult for us to hear truth and close us off from our inner voice and guidance.

I believe that the problem is not that we need more ways to communicate, but that we have to become better listeners. In all the noise and confusion, we have forgotten how to listen.

Imagine for a moment that you have a room full of people listening to a five minute talk on what it means to be happy. What would each person hear? It is likely that if you asked each person to tell the message they had heard, you would receive a different message from each.

The messages would be similar but different. Why? When people listen, how do they hear? Sometimes people listen through their fears. When they do they become afraid and react to imaginings and the unknown. Some people listen through their insecurities and they feel diminished, feeling that the words somehow have been directed at their inadequacies and lack of abilities. Some people listen through their expectations and they become disappointed and cynical. What they hear does not reflect the perfection that they had created in their minds and, therefore, the message is inadequate and somehow flawed. Some people listen through their anger and they become bitter. Some people listen through what they think they know and they deny themselves the truth.

Listening is a very special talent. It is an art form. Each one of us has to learn to remove the filters and learn to hear. It takes more than good ears to hear. It takes clarity of mind and clarity of the emotions to really hear. When really listening we hear with our emotions; we hear with our hearts; we hear with our Spirits. We feel the words. We learn to turn off all the noise and truly listen.

Listening is not easy but the rewards are great. It requires that we take responsibility and that we accept truth. When we listen through truth, we are freed and uplifted. Truth by its very nature is empowering for it allows us to make real choices and move forward. It frees us from our fears and the things that have held us back. Truth gives us tools such as compassion, awareness, insight, understanding, courage, and patience.

When we listen through compassion, we gain understanding and insight. When we listen through experience, we are reminded of the power of responsibility and choices in life. When we use experience positively, it can be a reassuring and empowering tool. When we allow experience to affect us negatively, we deny our ability to learn and become grounded in fear, anger, and insecurity. Reject the negative. When we listen through joy, we are filled with the awareness of wonderful possibilities.

Find a quiet spot and listen. Listen through your heart and open yourself to the world of Spirit and the love of God. Feel love in your heart and celebrate the wondrous life you have been given with all of its challenges and opportunities. Remember that you are connected to all and that you can learn to feel the words—to feel the truth. As you listen, you will become aware of the fact that words are not necessary.

Love is a force which animates the universe. It is through love that we can truly listen and gain peace. To embrace this truth is to transform the many ways we communicate into forces which will reaffirm the love and peace in our hearts. Celebrate your ability to listen today.

What Gift Do I Have?
How Will I be of Service?

The other day, a friend of mine was in a panic because it was the birthday of a loved one and as of yet, she hadn't found a gift. She had hunted through all the stores looking for that perfect gift. She had thought and thought and couldn't come up with anything. She had the money. She was desperate. She needed a gift so this person would know how much she loved him. Finally, she went to a store and didn't come home until she had something. Her task was done. She had a gift. A shiny, new thing to brighten up a birthday and to say I love you.

She didn't realize that even while she searched and searched, she already had a gift more precious and lasting than any bright, shiny thing she could buy in a store. The gift she had to share was the gift of her love—unconditional and joyous.

We often forget that we carry this special gift. We also forget that love is a coin that multiplies as we spend it. This means that we should never be stingy when dealing with love. We should share it freely and not save it for just a few or try to save it for a rainy day.

You have all felt the warmth of this gift in the form of a smile, a kind word, or maybe a word of support at a time when you needed it. These may have been times when you did not feel loved. These may have been times when you felt alone. If they were, and even if they were not, you were given a gift.

The gift of love is only given when you expect nothing in return. If you expect something in return, you are involved in commerce not love. Expecting something in return is selling your gift which, of course, means it is not a gift. Love is not for sale. It is given freely and without strings. Joy comes from both the giving and receiving of love. The joy comes from the knowledge that it is a gift given freely. How many of you have experienced the turmoil of love given and received with strings—with a price? Reject the strings, and free yourself. The same love without strings is joy. You deserve joy.

If the coin of Spirit is love, then it is spent through service. Each of us is called to serve. Each of us is called to share the coin of love. We do not all serve Spirit by standing on the platform sharing a lecture as I do or by demonstrating the gifts of Spirit. We are not all called to be doctors or counsellors. Whether you realize it or not, you do and can make a difference through service. You can all share a kind word, a smile, or a friendly gesture. You can all offer support and assistance to those in need. You minister to those around you each and every day. In the world today, if we look around, we can see many lost souls: those who are weary and confused; those who have lost their way; those who have found the foundations of their faith shattered; those who do not know where to turn; those who think they are alone and without hope. Share your gift with them. Be of service to them, for none are lost from the sight of God and you have been brought to them for a reason.

There are other lost souls who also need to know the gift of unconditional love. Many of these souls do not know they are lost. They need understanding and guidance. Wherever there are individuals clinging to falsity, to blindness, to intolerance, to superstition, to the dross of materialism, there is need for those who choose to be of service.

Remember, however, that it is not your will you wish to impose on another. It is not your mission to force a truth onto another. Understanding and faith must come from within, so share your truth and let go. Help others find their gift to share and receive. Belief without understanding is like love without freedom—empty. Each person will come to the Light in his or her own time. Each person must move along the path to their own understanding.

Share your gift. Watch it grow and blossom. Fill yourself with joy and celebrate—for you have chosen a path of service and you have chosen the way of Spirit. God has blessed you.

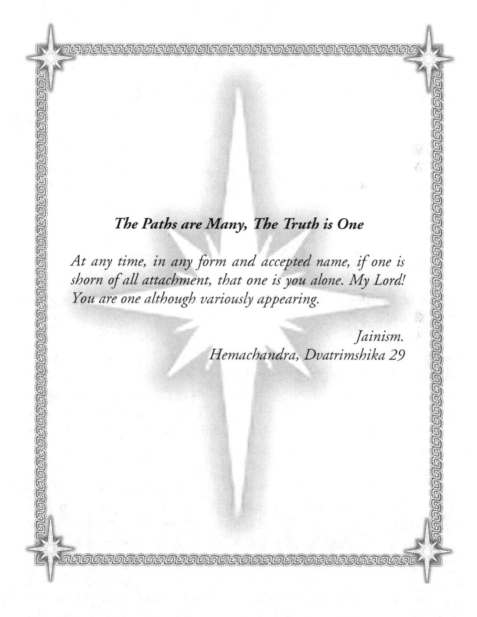

The Paths are Many, The Truth is One

At any time, in any form and accepted name, if one is shorn of all attachment, that one is you alone. My Lord! You are one although variously appearing.

Jainism.
Hemachandra, Dvatrimshika 29

We Are All Shepherds

We are all shepherds. A shepherd to me is someone who is gentle, kind, thoughtful and compassionate. A shepherd is someone who would risk his or her life for another who is weak or helpless. A shepherd loves and respects all living things.

We have been given a sacred trust. We have been made caretakers of what must be one of the most diverse and beautiful places in the universe. Ancient peoples recognized this trust and accepted it. They spoke of Mother Earth and treated their mother with the utmost of respect and love.

Today, we have dominion over all living things. The test of our ability as the shepherd comes from how we use it. As a race, we have failed to show the qualities of the shepherd. Many look upon nature as an adversary to be bent to our will. We have worked very hard to isolate ourselves from the natural world. In doing so, we have also removed ourselves from an important connection to our Mother, Father, God.

It has not always been that way. Many aboriginal peoples believed that all things had a spirit—the trees, the animals, the rocks, and the wind—all things. They did not own property because how could another own a living thing and in truth the concept of ownership was not well developed in their society.

In New Brunswick, for example, when the Mik'maq killed a moose, it was done with great respect. Thanks was given for they recognized that this animal had given its life for their continued existence. They killed only when there was need and they used everything. For example, from a moose: they ate the meat; they used the hide for clothing and leather; the brain was used for tanning hides; the bones became tools; the powdered hoofs were used as a cure for epilepsy; the antlers were used for medicine; the gut made snowshoe bindings and thread for sewing; the long hairs on the chin were used for embroidery; and the shin bones were used to make dice. Nothing was wasted.

Even the pioneers who fought nature had an understanding of their connection to it. They believed that God had placed plants on the earth for man's benefit and to determine the use of the plant you had merely to look at it. This was known as the Doctrine of Signatures. A plant that looked like the heart was good for heart ailments.

Both of these peoples drew their survival directly from their environment. The aboriginal people and the pioneers recognized the source for their continued physical existence. It was Mother Earth. Being practical, they understood they were connected to that source and to abuse it, put it and them, at risk. They could not have imagined how far from that source we could move nor how much at risk we could place our world.

Often we can be overwhelmed by the size of environmental issues. Not only are they difficult to understand but we feel helpless to do anything to resolve them. The journey to change begins with the first step. I have seen ants move what to them would be mountains of soil, one grain at a time. Let us approach environmental issues like the ant. Let us be conscious and aware. Let us become informed. Why don't we do what we can do? For example, do not be discouraged into inaction about all the styrofoam cups in the world destroying our ozone layer and causing cancer in our unborn children. Just don't buy that cup of coffee in a styrofoam cup, and share your feelings with others.

Do what you can do today. The path is made of many small steps. If you do not start now being a shepherd for this imperilled earth, when will the journey begin and how will you finish the task?

I do not believe that we will destroy our planet because I see more and more people taking responsibility and I see the signs of change. Change for the good will only happen if each of us does our small part. Together we are legion and we will succeed. When I look at the beauty of a sunset or marvel at a flower, I want to know that today I have done what I can do to ensure that this miracle we call home with all of its diversity is in the hands of love. I want to know that the good shepherd in all of us has been awakened and that we have nurtured our home until it is green again.

We are all shepherds.

On Angel's Wings
Transformational Encounters with Spirit!

A Christmas Angel

This true experience was shared with us by a woman from Charlottetown. It is one of my favourite Christmas stories to share. Rev Barry

Will you please try to visualize the layout of my home? It is a two story, Cape Cod with four rooms on the lower level—a kitchen and den at the back of the house and a living room and formal dining room across the front.

The living room is warmly decorated for yet another Christmas Eve. As I stand and look at the tree, with its lopsided ornaments and lights, I am overwhelmed by feelings of sadness and quite a bit of anger. My three children, ages 5, 7 and 9 and I had hours of fun decorating this tree, writing letters to Santa and preparing lunch for him again this year. Now it is time to assemble the toys, fill the socks, etc.

Again this year, the children's father has promised to stay sober and help with this task. He is dead to the world and loudly snoring and sleeping it off in the den. I look at the toys, one in particular—a small pool table for my youngest son that needs to be assembled. Other things need to be arranged or assembled, as well. Again, I stand alone with this task. I will admit that I felt like just leaving things the way they were and let the children awake to a different Christmas. Of course, I would not. I looked out the window to see the big soft flakes of snow falling. There was not a breeze. The night was exceptionally peaceful and calm. Tears started falling and I began to feel sorry for myself.

There was a knock at the front door. I opened it to face a young man of about 30 with fair hair and a tweed suit jacket. He stated that he had just run his car off the road down the street and asked if he could use the phone. It was not uncommon for cars to miss the turn at the end of our street. I told him the telephone was in the kitchen. I was a bit nervous about allowing a stranger into my home at 1:30 A.M. so I told him my husband was resting on the couch and to try not to disturb him. As if anything could disturb him in his state!

Then he left. The lights were out in the dining room, so I strolled in there to watch him walk away. As you may have guessed, I saw nothing. There were no footprints in the new fallen snow and no one to be seen. I grabbed my boots and went outside into the most beautiful night. I ran to the spot where he told me he had gone into the ditch. There was no car and no signs of tracks on the street. I was not frightened. I was feeling confused but strangely, very much at peace. I went back home and called the only place I knew to be open on Christmas Eve. The man at the Government Garage said he had received no call asking for a tow truck.

I slept and awoke very rested. We enjoyed a wonderful Christmas. I told no one this story and months went by. Another Christmas was on the horizon and early Christmas Eve, as I walked by the telephone, I instinctively picked it up—it did not ring—and it was the voice of that young man who helped me the previous Christmas. All he said was . . . "do you need me this year?" My response was a very quiet and grateful "no, thank you, not this year." He called every year on Christmas Eve until my youngest son reached the age of 14.

God sent me an angel. I will always feel so blessed.

TUESDAY
WEDNESDAY
THURSDAY
FRIDAY
2
3
4
5
6
9
10
11
12
13
16
18
19
20
22
23
29
30
31
P. John Burden

Today is the Tomorrow You Hoped for Yesterday

The other day I asked myself, "Why are so many people unhappy?" Why is it that people have such a difficult time basking in the joys and wonder that the world has to offer? As I thought, Spirit gave me a phrase, *"Today is the tomorrow you hoped for yesterday."*

A long time ago, people struggled from day to day just to survive. At that time, each day was very precious because it meant that you had survived another day. It was also precious because there might be no tomorrow. Each time they met an old friend, enjoyed the touch of a loved one, ate a meal, saw a sunset—they were thankful. They knew it might be the last time they enjoyed these simple pleasures on this earth. They felt close to God. God was in the present. God was in the trees, the oceans, the rocks, and all living things. They had few possessions to occupy and clutter their minds or to worry about. They were happy. They prospered. They developed society and culture.

Today in North America, most of us no longer worry about our day to day survival. Most of us know that we will eat tomorrow. We know that chances are good that we will live to see another day. We have a lot of time to think. How do we use this time? Do we try to help those who are not sure of their next meal? Do we use it in service to others? Do we use it to develop and nurture friendships and loving relationships?

Sometimes, we use our time unproductively. We take this precious time for granted. Often we spend the time worrying about what we don't have! Worrying about the things of the past which we cannot change! Fearing those things in the future that we cannot see!

I would like to share with you the story of the man who walking along one day heard a roaring and growling coming up behind him. Looking back, he saw that he was being stalked by a tiger. This tiger began to pounce, so the man, with every ounce of strength he could muster, began to run. In a few moments, with the tiger getting closer and closer, he found himself looking over a steep cliff. With little choice, he began to climb down the cliff. As he looked up, he could see the tiger looking over the edge—growling and roaring. The man knew that if the tiger could reach him, he would surely die. At about half way down the cliff, the man heard a roaring and growling from below. Looking down, he saw that there was another tiger waiting for him at the bottom of the cliff. At that moment, the man realized that whether he climbed up or down the cliff he would have to face a tiger. He would probably die. All of a sudden, the man saw a strawberry growing on an outcropping of the cliff. It was red and ripe and luscious. As the man could reach it, he reached over and picked the strawberry. He then ate it, and enjoyed it. Even though, the man was facing certain disaster at both the top and bottom of the cliff, he was able to live in the moment and enjoy the strawberry.

How many of us have tigers at the top of the cliff in our past and imagine tigers in our future at the bottom of the cliff? How many of us can live in the moment and enjoy what life has to offer now? How many of us know joy in our lives?

Imagine that God is the strawberry—A God of the present. Spirit lives in an eternal now and so should we. Faith has to do with living in the now and being positive—celebrating our gifts. Like the man on the cliff, we can gain nourishment and joy from the strawberry. That does not mean that we should ignore the things of the past or the possibilities for the future. It does mean, however, that these things should not have the power to rob us of the joy of the moment.

Let us live our lives to their fullest, doing the best that we can do and being content that we have done our best. No one, especially God, expects us to do better than we can in this moment. We all make mistakes. We are not perfect. That is why we are here—to make mistakes, to learn, to grow, to move towards perfection. The frustrating thing about perfection is that the closer we get to it, the farther away it goes. The more we know, the more we know that we do not know. Do the best you can and be thankful that you have been given an opportunity to live on this wonderful planet and experience the challenges that a life can bring to you.

Know that each day is a growing day and that today is the tomorrow you wished for yesterday. Use it well! Enjoy it!

Life is Purposeful

The other day I was talking to someone who wanted to know what their soul's purpose was in this life. They felt that they had been searching for a long time and they were concerned that they might not find it or achieve it. They had tried many things but none of them brought the happiness or the fulfilment they felt that achieving that special task should bring them. They hoped that I could contact their Spirit guides and ask them what it was that they had set out to accomplish in this life. Spirit was able to give them relevant direction and guidance but fell short of telling them what their soul's purpose was in this life. I thought I would share with you some of the reasons why Spirit would choose not to tell them.

I believe our lives are very purposeful and that we come into this life with specific goals and tasks to achieve. I also believe we chose the family and the situation that we were born into. This enables us to have the experiences and circumstances necessary to provide the opportunities and challenges we need to achieve what we set out to do in this life. It is important to understand that achieving the goals we set for ourselves is only meaningful if we achieve them without the awareness that we must. To do something because you have to is quite different than doing something because it is natural or right. I believe that it is necessary for us to accomplish our soul's purposes or goals through right actions not because it is set out as a task that we must accomplish. This is one of the reasons why we do not remember what our goals are in this life.

Sometimes when life seems incomprehensible and we feel lost, it would be reassuring to be able to open the book and check the page that tells us where we should be and what we should be doing at that time. But life is to be lived and the how we find our way is by making choices that move us towards happiness and fulfilment. Choices are often not easy but they provide the new opportunities we need to learn and grow in meaningful ways. It has been my experience that we do not make mistakes on our journey because whatever choice we make is grounded in our current awareness. Whatever challenge it brings to us is the opportunity we need to learn some special thing. If we choose to learn it, then we will never need to have that challenge again. There are no short cuts and knowing our soul's purpose does not change the need we have to experience and learn. The journey through life is a spiritual one because it is a journey made through our awareness of self and our need to grow and become.

A few years ago, two friends discovered that the "talking board" was their natural way to channel information from the Spirit side. One of the sessions that came through seemed particularly relevant to this question. Spirit titled it "The Many Roads to Happiness." It reads . . .

> *Know that life can have many different roads to happiness. There are many ways in which we are needed. The paths to any of these can lead to an exciting and fulfilling life.*
>
> *The fork in the road we choose does not have to be right or wrong. You can often choose between the things that would provide happiness in different areas. When we think there is only one thing or person that can make us happy, we are putting limits on the God force within us. We are limitless, but by our own choosing, we can stay limited and powerless. This is usually done in ignorance of any other knowledge.*
>
> *The knowledge is available—we have only to open our eyes and ears. The Spirit within us that wants happiness is the force that makes us see and hear. The lessons get deeper as our understanding progresses. Think hard on this lesson. It is a timely one.*

I often feel that we are limiting ourselves when we search for a simple answer for our reason for being here in this life. We have been blessed with the opportunity to live in a wondrously diverse and beautiful place. In this life, every day, we realize many goals and accomplish many things. Each life, each day presents us with opportunities to grow in new and exciting ways. If we believe that life is purposeful, then we should also believe that we are here in each life to achieve not one thing, but many things. We must listen and trust the wisdom of our higher self to get it right.

I remember a number of years ago a young man who from a very young age knew the face of his future bride. He felt a connection to this woman from a previous life and had met her in this life only through dreams. This knowledge limited his ability to live a normal and happy life because any other woman he met was not his true love. Until he met her, he was destined to be lonely and unhappy. This awareness affected his ability to make choices. It may have even negatively affected his chances of meeting or being happy with this woman when he met her since he had not experienced a normal social life because of his awareness. This is an extreme case but it does illustrate how we can restrict ourselves from the many opportunities and choices we have in life. When we do, this life's possibilities are diminished and we no longer live in a limitless world.

Even though there is in my mind no question that life is purposeful, we must remain open to the many opportunities to grow and learn that life offers us. As the Spirit reading says *there are many roads to happiness.* Know that when you come to the fork in the road whatever choice you make will take you to a greater understanding of yourself and of your journey. Let right actions be your guide and strive to be happy.

The Paths are Many, The Truth is One

*Those who believe in the Qur'an, those who follow
the Jewish scriptures, and the Sabeans and the
Christians—any who believe in God and the Last Day,
and work righteousness—on them shall be no fear, nor
shall they grieve.*

*Islam.
Qur'an 5.69*

Who's Life is it?

The other day, I was speaking to someone about the difference between free will and destiny. There are many who believe that the major events in our lives are pre-ordained and unchangeable. They believe destiny or fate controls their future and that no matter what they do they cannot change it.

Now let's take a minute and think about this. To me, this notion that things are unchangeable presents a serious problem. If you have no control over the events in your life, then what is the point of a life? If you are merely a puppet going through the motions, then why bother with the motions? How can we make choices? How can we grow?

I have met a number of people who have learned in their tradition that if they do something wrong God will punish them. These same people have had their faith shattered by the fact that when something bad happens in their lives they feel they are being punished for something they must have done. Because they do not understand, they turn away from God—A God of Love—at a time when they need God the most.

If you add the notion that if you do something wrong God will punish you, to the notion that fate/destiny dictates the events in your life, the picture can become pretty depressing. Now you are being punished for doing things that apparently you have no choice but to do. It is little wonder that so many people are depressed, unhappy and confused!

I have some good and some bad news for you.

The good news is that the myths about destiny are not true. It is not true that you have no control over your life. You live in a free will universe. You are not only in control of your life. You are the master of your future. You are in a physical life to make choices and to grow.

It is also not true that God punishes you when you make a mistake. You grow by learning from the choices you make. When you make a bad choice it takes you down a path of learning which hopefully will help you make a better choice in the future. If you do not learn, you will probably make the same bad choice and be given yet another opportunity to choose more wisely. Since God is a loving God and wants you to be happy, you will have as many opportunities as you need to get it right. God wants you to grow.

You have been given a wonderful gift, a life on this beautiful planet. This life is yours to do with as you wish. To not have free will would be like being given a car as a gift only so that you could drive the giver wherever he or she wanted to go.

It is true that when you came into this life you entered with a number of tasks which may have included the opportunity to accomplish or experience certain things. If you believe in karma, there may also be debts you have to pay back to others. You may have asked to experience helplessness, or great love, or compassion, or any one of a hundred other things.

You have Spirit guides to provide support and guidance from the other side. These Spirits are there because before you came into this life you asked some of your Spirit friends who had mastered the qualities that you wish to work on to give you guidance and support from the other side. Even though you may not be aware of it, Spirit speaks to you every day. You have guidance and you are never alone.

All the things in your life are there because while you were in the Spirit world before your birth into the physical you chose them. You chose your parents. You chose the circumstances into which you would be born. The choices you made were the ones which would provide you with the greatest opportunity to accomplish the tasks that you have set for yourself in this life.

When you come into this life, your memories of your Spirit-life are hidden from you. This means that you do not remember that you are eternal nor why you came into the physical. It is important that when we come into the physical, we do not remember what those tasks are because if we knew what they were and we knew that there is a wonderful life for us in the world of Spirit, we would busy ourselves with the tasks we had come to accomplish and once finished, leave. It is also important because if you know you have to be nice or loving or kind because you are afraid of what will happen to you if you are not, there is little benefit for you. You have to do things because they are right—not because you have to.

Many people believe that when you have a psychic or Spiritual reading all the things that are talked about in the future are absolute—unchangeable. Some believe a psychic is accurate only if everything happens just as he or she said it would. To understand guidance from Spirit is to understand that this is not true. If it were true, why would Spirit bother to tell you?—To prove how accurate they can be? The whole point of a reading is to empower you to make changes in your life. If you do not like what you are told about the future, then it is your job to change it. Spirit sees a number of possible futures. Spirit can tell you what will happen if you continue to move along the same path you are now on. A reading can put you on notice that it is time to change. Whether you do or not is up to you.

A number of years ago, a man and his wife came to me for a reading. When doing the reading for the man's wife, Spirit noted that she had been having chest pains and suggested that she knew it was time for her to visit a doctor as soon as possible. Spirit told her that she knew she had heart problems over the last year and that it was not something she should take lightly. The woman assured me that she would visit the doctor on Monday when the office opened. Spirit reiterated that she should not forget. The husband said he would make sure that she did not forget. Spirit accepted this and continued with the reading. A week later, I received a call from the husband who was devastated. The woman had not gone to the doctor on the Monday and on the Friday had died of a massive heart attack. She had made a choice.

One of the hardest lessons for most of us to accept is that the only life that we have the power to change is our own. Sometimes when we feel we have the answers, we try to save others from the pain of going through the consequences of a wrong choice. You cannot accept the responsibility for anyone else's choices and you certainly should not make their choices for them. To attempt to live another's life is to rob them of their opportunity to make choices and grow. If you make their choices for them, then you have sentenced them to the task of finding another opportunity to learn the lesson that you have just robbed them of. That is not to say that many people are not more than happy to let you live their lives for them. It is easier! It is safer! And if it doesn't go right, then they can blame you. The other problem in trying to save people from difficult times is that you do not know what experiences they need to go through in this life.

It's important to note that a reading will never tell you exactly what you should do. To do so would be to rob you of the opportunity to choose. The reading will tell you some of the things to consider around the issue and provide you with insight into it. Spirit will reaffirm what you already know and offer you support in your decisions.

YOU are the master of YOUR future. That does not mean that YOU will not have to go through some things YOU would rather not GO THROUGH, but it does mean that you can accept responsibility for what you do go through and learn from it.

What is the bad news? Well, the bad news is also good news if you accept the challenge of a physical existence. You cannot blame God or the devil or anyone else for the choices you make in your life. Any challenges you face or have faced are ones you have chosen and you can rejoice for you will succeed in facing and overcoming them. You are growing and you are experiencing a free will universe. You are here in the life you are living because you have chosen it. Celebrate the opportunities it is providing for you.

I guess for some there is further bad news. Some people find this news most difficult to deal with while others will embrace it with joy. What is this news? It is that we are responsible for our lives and for translating what we believe into action. Take charge of your lives and celebrate the wonderful gift that you have been given. You are not only eternal but you are privileged to have the gift of a physical existence. How will you choose to use it?

Action is the Fuel of Life

When I started thinking about what I would write, I wasn't quite sure just what to say. As I often do, I took a moment and asked Spirit for some guidance. I was suddenly aware of places and people pregnant with ideas. I could see situations and people brimming with possibilities. I could see people asking Spirit for guidance and receiving answers. I could see people praying and being brought opportunities in answer to their prayers. Even though I could see all these wonderful things, there was something missing. Something was wrong with the picture that I saw. People were not happy. Situations were not being resolved. Opportunities were amounting to nothing. What was missing? What was the key?

The missing key was action—a simple word but one of great power. It is only through action that possibilities—that thoughts are translated from intent, from the etheric into the physical. It is only through action that we are able to move ourselves through life with awareness. That means that we are in charge of our lives and action is the affirmation that puts us squarely in the driver's seat. Without action, things do not get resolved through conscious choice. Without action, seeds do not blossom.

It is important we understand that a spiritual journey is a journey of seeking truth and translating that truth into action. Once we have undertaken action, we can reassess the situation by examining the consequences. Once the consequences are assessed, we continue our search. The path is a path of patience and courage. It is a process which is never completed because we will always strive for greater truth and awareness.

I have seen people spend a great deal of time trying to find answers only to be stopped by inaction once they have them. If we ask Spirit for guidance, we must be prepared to take that information and translate it into action. Knowledge without action is empty.

There are many reasons for inaction. Sometimes people are not prepared to face change. Sometimes the thing we hate is something familiar—sort of comfortable—and therefore very hard to let go of. Sometimes we are not prepared to face truth. Sometimes we are afraid. Sometimes we are waiting for someone else to act. No matter what the reason for our inaction, know that it is only through action that we can move forward. God wants us to be happy but we must choose through action to realize the possibilities which are brought to us.

Sometimes right action can make us feel uncomfortable or unhappy because it challenges us. Challenges are not a bad thing. We may be reacting to newness, or change, or may be moved to more right action which will move us forward.

It is also important to know that when we choose no action, it is considered action. Not to act on truth is a choice to act or remain in untruth. So if we ask for truth, receive it and have not acted, then our choice of action was to ignore the truth. Non-action is an action by default and has real consequences.

Action born out of fear or impatience is not action through truth. There are many who allow fear to be the impetus that moves them through their lives. Fear of being alone, fear of upsetting someone else, fear of making a mistake, fear of accepting responsibility, fear of living, fear of dying are all motivators for inaction or wrong action. Do not allow fear to move you to action or bring you to inaction. Happiness and love do not come from untruths such as fear. Fear is the mind killer. Fear serves no function except to rob your power from you. You are of Spirit and you have nothing to fear.

God does not expect any of us to change overnight. Action does not necessarily need to be drastic or overly challenging. Take one step at a time. There is no need to be overwhelmed. Each step will move us closer to truth. Each step will move us closer to happiness. Rejoice that we have the tools to achieve our goals—even when we do not know what they are. Know that the fuel which will move us through life is action based on truth—action based on love. With truth as our fuel, we will move through our challenges filled with joy and light. We will succeed.

Why Am I Here?

We are on this earth to build our characters. It is the way we face our challenges that build this character. Remember there is no power in this world that is greater than our power—the power within us. Our challenges and troubles are of the earth plane—the physical, and we are of the world of Spirit—of God.

Everything we have in the world of form can have a price. The price of mediumship is increased sensitivity. The price of knowledge is responsibility. The price of wealth is the possibility of forgetting our duties to Spirit. Learning to accept and understand the price of things—of choices—is part of the Spiritual path.

We must learn to explore the riches within ourselves and reveal the diamonds of Spirit that are within the clay of our natures. We all possess these riches for we are part of the God Essence.

Faith, that is faith alone, sometimes fails when the winds of bitter experience blow. Faith born out of knowledge provides a foundation that is so strong that no wind can disturb or dislodge it. Blessed are those who believe and have not seen, but thrice blessed are those who know, and because they know, place their faith in that which is not yet revealed to them. They know that the laws of the universe are operating by the power which is love and wisdom.

We should all have absolute faith because it is a faith born out of knowledge. We have proof of the power and reality of Spirit. We should know that whether we understand it or not, the world is unfolding as it should. Trust that we will make the right decisions for our greater good and that we will weather the storms which are a natural part of life.

Banish all thought that negativity or evil can touch us. We live under the protection of the Light of God and God's Universal Laws. The power that envelops us, the power that supports and seeks to guide us and inspire us is the power of the God Essence. This power can sustain us through our trials and difficulties.

Peace and joy is found within. It is not found outside of ourselves. Look within and we will find joy. We will find the God of our understanding. We will find faith. We will find comfort. Do not judge eternity with the eyes of the physical. Do not judge the parts until we have seen the whole.

The Paths are Many, The Truth is One

There can be no doubt that whatever the peoples of
the world, of whatever race or religion, they derive
their inspiration from one Heavenly Source, and are
the subjects of one God. The difference between the
ordinances under which they abide should be attributed
to the varying requirements and exigencies of the age
in which they were revealed. All of them, except for a
few which are the outcome of human perversity, were
ordained of God, and are a reflection of His Will and
Purpose.

Baha'i Faith.
Gleanings from the Writings of Baha'u'llah 111

And I (Jesus) have other sheep, that are not of this fold;
I must bring them also, and they will heed my voice. So
there shall be one flock, one shepherd.

Christianity.
Bible, John 10.16

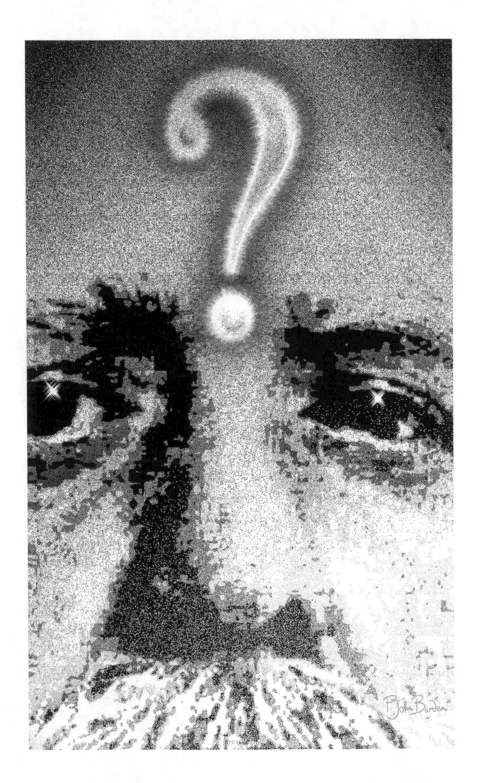

The Spiritual Path is a Path of Questions

The other day, someone came to me with a number of questions regarding Spirit. They began the conversation by apologizing for asking questions and said that they had hesitated to bother me with them. I reassured them that I was happy to help answer any questions they might have, if I could. I was also quick to point out to them that I, too, was once filled with questions about Spirit and was thankful for the support of those who helped me find my answers. I reminded them that asking questions is part of the spiritual journey and the day they have no questions will be the day that they step off their Spiritual path. This conversation prompted me to write this and to title it, "The Spiritual path is a path of questions."

Let me begin by saying, "People who do not ask questions have not yet stepped onto the Spiritual path." It is through questioning and testing that we find answers. It is by pushing the boundaries of our understanding that we gain knowledge. It is by being sceptical that we eliminate deception and build strong foundations. Never apologize for asking questions and needing confirmation. It is today that you are building the foundations to help you when times are difficult or when your understanding is tested.

Many people are asked to embrace a concept of God and Spirit which does not allow them to ask questions. They have learned that to ask questions is to question the word of God. They have learned that God will "fix" their lives if they embrace the doctrine without question.

These people do not understand that the Spiritual path is a path of tests and challenges. These people do not expect to be tested. They do not expect difficult times. When faced with life's challenges or when faced with difficult times, they turn from God because they feel that they are being punished unjustly or that God is unfairly allowing bad things to happen to them.

Our faith must be tempered with questioning and discernment. Building strong foundations requires that we explore our faith and understanding with awareness. Strong foundations allow us to weather life's challenges and grow. Such foundations are also a source of strength for others when there is need.

Some people reject the existence of God and Spirit without seeking answers. They cannot understand it, so therefore it cannot be. These people embody the negative aspect of scepticism. Scepticism is a good thing when it moves us to find answers and gain understanding. Many, however, allow the belief in nothing to be their doctrine—their religion. They ask questions without seeking answers. This is a type of ignorance which is very difficult to see for often it is hidden behind the questions. To ask questions without the courage to seek the truth and change your understanding when faced with answers is to lie to one's self. It does not provide a foundation from which to build understanding.

Humanity has been blessed with many teachers of Spiritual truth. They have taught us much about love and responsibility. Gaining knowledge and understanding is a process. It incorporates both internal and external dimensions. To gain knowledge of Spirit, we must listen with both our physical ears and our intuition. Spirit speaks to us. God speaks to us from both the physical world and our inner world.

We must be patient and learn to listen.

Each of us stands on a threshold. Each of us stands between the two worlds. Some have embraced the reality of Spirit. Many of us can testify to its existence. Many of us are asking questions and finding answers. As we find answers, our understanding and insight has its foundations in the concrete—in the physical.

As we work with Spirit and ask questions, we develop our own personal proof. Why is this important? Why is it necessary to work with Spirit in concrete ways? After all, doesn't Spirit work in everyone's life even if they do not embrace the reality of the Heaven World and the ability to communicate with it?

It is important to develop our own personal proof and work with Spirit because for each of us:

- 👁 Exploring our connections to Spirit allows us to gain knowledge and understanding. It gives us insight into the ways we experience the manifestations of Spirit in the physical.

- 👁 Developing our gifts gives us our own personal proof as to the presence of the unseen world and the reality of God in our lives.

- 👁 Through an understanding of the ways of Spirit, we learn to accept responsibility for our choices. God does not live our lives for us. We can accept responsibility for our successes and failures. We can accept the credit for our growth and can thank God for the opportunities.

- 👁 Spirit work confirms the reality of God and the certain knowledge that we are all eternal.

- 👁 Understanding the reality of the Spirit realms and the challenges of the Spiritual path can help us gain insight and understanding from the events in our lives. Having an understanding of the Spirit realms can help us to make the choices which move us along the path for our greatest good even when that path is full of difficult challenges.

- 👁 We come to understand that there are many paths to God's light and truth. To understand the nature of Spirit is to understand that God is love and that it is this love that infuses all traditions with God's Light. Loving people from all traditions will stand together in the world of Spirit. They will rejoice in the knowledge that God has created many paths along which souls can travel to reach the Light.

- Working with and coming to understand Spirit provides us with opportunities and hopefully the desire to be of service.

How can it help others that we ask questions and develop our own personal proofs and work with Spirit:

- It provides a place where people can go who have questions and are seeking answers.

- It broadens the foundations of insight and understanding from which others can learn.

- Working with Spirit provides opportunities for God's Light to manifest in the physical through us.

- It provides opportunities for those seeking truth to have their experiences validated in concrete ways.

- It allows us to share a broader understanding of God and Spirit with others who have a narrower perspective. It promotes love, tolerance, inclusiveness and compassion.

- It helps people with their transition into the Spirit world.

Spirit Speaks
Messages shared through Spirit-Medium
Rev. Barry King

The following excerpt from a "Spirit Channelling Session" on February 27, 2003 with one of our regular groups. (*The process is relatively easy and natural for an experienced medium. It is without dramatics and most often very quiet and gentle. I do not go into a trance but I do achieve an altered state which allows me to step aside and let Spirit work through me. Our sessions are taped and the following is not edited or modified but is written exactly as it was spoken.*)

Session facilitator: *You may share your wisdom with us?*

Guide 2 speaking through Barry: Wisdom is a fleeting thing, my child.

Do you have a message for us as a group?

I shall share my humble offerings. Be assured that no one stands alone; it is the challenge of those who retain a glimmer of their Spirit essence, a glimmer of memory of their spirit life to feel alone. For in the physical, you are separated through perception from not only the Source but also your connection to all others. I use the word perception, for that separation is but an illusion. You are not separated.

You are not alone. You exist in perfection, but surrounded by illusion. You exist as an individual, but you are part of the body. You are not alone. We stand with you. We are connected to you. We support you and we assist you in the task that you have set for yourself.

In the time that you have in the physical—this time is fleeting—there is so much to do, so much to accomplish. Separated from the memory, it is hard sometimes to know whether you are on track, whether you move along the path or whether you will get caught and become immobile. Each of you, here in this room, is moving along the path. Each of you, in part because of your special perception and understanding, feels more alone. For it is when we know what being connected to the Source means that we begin to understand the feeling of separation.

You each should congratulate yourselves for the courage it takes to move along the path and know that each of you has achieved much, even though there are days, and more days than we wish to acknowledge, that we feel we have accomplished little. Understand that much is hidden from you. Understand that this is how it must be. It has been said that a little knowledge is a dangerous thing. Ignorance has also been called bliss, for not knowing is, to many, a great escape, and not understanding, nor accepting responsibility is also a great escape. Those who are grounded in awareness and strive to move along the path can only hope to achieve that which they have set out to do. But the gift is the awareness that there is so much more. That there is much that moves below the surface of one's awareness, and that one can in time learn to connect with that. We on the Spirit side, we guides and supporters of those immersed in the physical, are diligent in our attempt to bring support to those who feel alone—not because they do not know but because they do. It is my pleasure to speak to you this evening but be assured that I speak to each of you in the moments when you need to know that there is someone there to offer some support.

Understand that the price one pays for awareness is awareness which means that you are not able to live the illusion and learn to be honest with yourself and celebrate your journey. We rejoice in the opportunities that you have to grow.

The Face in the Mirror

I have come across a poem I had cut out a number of years ago. The poem has a valuable message to share.

The Face in the Mirror

When you get what you want in your struggle for self
And the world makes you king for a day.
Just go to the mirror and look at yourself
And see what that face has to say.
For it isn't your father, or mother or spouse
Whose judgement upon you must pass.
The person whose verdict counts most in your life
Is the one staring back from the glass.

Some people might think you're a straight shooting chum
And call you a great gal or guy
But the face in the glass says you're only a bum;
If you can't look it straight in the eye.
You may fool the whole world down the pathway of years
And get pats on the back as you pass
But the final reward will be heartache and tears
If you've cheated the face in the glass.

That's the one you must please, never mind all the rest
That's the one with you clear to the end.
And you know you have passed the most dangerous test
If the face in the glass is your friend

Anonymous

When I first read this poem, I was struck by its simple truth. In the Interfaith Ministry, one of the things we teach is the power of our thoughts. It is important for us to realize that our thoughts about others can often be influenced by our thoughts about ourselves. Therefore one of the places we must begin to work is with our perception of ourselves. That's why the mirror can be so useful.

Where do we start? I believe the best place to start when we look at ourselves is to look at our intent. Why we do what we do? If actions are done for the wrong reasons, we may transform a loving act into something else. Actions may be transformed if they create guilt, or dependency. Remember, we are not measured by our deeds but by our thoughts which are grounded in our intention. A controlling act which appears to be an act of love is still a controlling act and is grounded in fear and negativity.

If we look deeper, we can see some of the ways that a lack of positive intent can manifest itself. It should also be noted that often times this is not done with malice but arises from a learned or unconscious behaviour. We all know people who appear very supportive or very loving or very spiritual, only to discover that these false emotions were used to control and manipulate. Sometimes the emotions are real, but the person cannot accept responsibility. Conscious or unconscious, these behaviours are by nature always destructive to both the person giving and the person receiving. They enable and perpetuate dysfunction.

Sometimes people act from insecurity. They have a difficult time looking into the mirror. Because they are unable to deal with their own issues, they spend all their time and energy trying to fix others. I had someone once tell me that they felt they should be a counsellor because they had been in counselling for many years. Even though they had chosen not to deal with the issues which brought them to see a counsellor, they felt they had nothing left to learn. When someone who has not faced their issues counsels others, they often create dependency, fear or confusion. We published an article some time ago called 'Co-dependency—the disease of good people.' Co-dependency is created by insecurity, and even though the conscious intent is positive, the underlying unconscious intent is grounded in negative emotions and fear.

Sometimes what bothers us when we look in the mirror is the fact that we did not offer constructive criticism. We allowed ourselves to react out of a negative emotion under the guise of constructive criticism and in doing so we hurt another. It can be particularly difficult when we use this mask to allow ourselves to be hurtful while telling ourselves that it is helping the other person. To face the mirror, we must learn to work through love.

We must balance our needs with the needs of others to be able to face the mirror. We must approach life through balance and work through love—love of ourselves and love for others. That does not mean we should be self-involved. It does mean that we should treat all living things with respect. I have seen good people be cruel and unfeeling in the guise of clarity. These people placed their needs and their wants above all others. Reject this trap.

The face in the mirror can only smile if you have earned your love. If you treat kindness and love as a commodity, you will have a difficult time with the mirror. When you offer something, it must be offered freely with no strings attached.

Our ego is precious and wonderful. It can help us not be victims and can promote a sense of happiness and well-being. Sometimes, however, people become so grounded in their ego that they cannot celebrate others' successes. Sometimes they try to undo others' good work because they themselves did not do it. Have you ever known anyone like that? Someone who puts others down to raise themselves up? Reject their negativity and do not get caught up in their dysfunction.

The issue with ego arises when we feel the need to be greater than others and to be special or stand above the crowd. Ego can become delusion and delusion can become very destructive. What we do must be grounded in reality, not ego. Through the Interfaith Ministry we try to instil in people the knowledge that we are all special, that life is purposeful, and we must reject that which is not grounded in reason.

Someone told me once of a man she had talked to who was very spiritual. He used to meditate for six to eight hours a day and had told her that he was going to move onto a higher level soon because he had nothing left to learn here. Beware of people who have nothing to learn. They are not good listeners.

What is the greatest challenge to master that will allow us to face the mirror? The challenge is honesty. When we are dishonest with ourselves and do not follow a path of truth, we have difficulty looking in the mirror. Choose a path of truth and love and stand before the mirror. You are your greatest critic and when you move into the next life you will have much to celebrate if you have been honest to the face in the mirror. You will learn from the mirror as it reflects your truth. Choose to grow through knowledge. Be all you can be and know that we are all sparks of the one Light, of the one truth. In time, we will all stand before the mirror as beautiful shining beings of Light.

The Chaos of Life is an Illusion!

Every spring, I am struck by the way that the miracle of resurrection—of rebirth is reflected in our daily lives. Spring is a time of year that we look forward to with anticipation. It is a time when we celebrate new life. For those of the Christian tradition, Easter celebrates the resurrection of Christ. For those of the Wiccan and Earth-based traditions, spring is also a time of renewal and rebirth.

Each spring, the natural world around us goes through a rebirth. From an apparently barren landscape, life bursts forth in a multitude of forms. Seeds germinate producing a new generation of plants which grow and prosper, reaching up towards the light of the sun. These plants in turn nourish a new generation of organisms each contributing to the diversity, order and well-being of the world we live in.

Maybe the world around you appears to be filled with chaos. Maybe your life appears to be filled with chaos. If we could step back and look at the larger picture, we would see order in the chaos. We would see that the chaos is an illusion. We live in an orderly universe. Our perception of this order is limited by our understanding and our perception. Whether we know it or not, there is order in our lives.

The image I hold to remind me of this order is the image of Christ, standing above the waters, calm and at peace while the storm rages around him. His peace comes from faith and an understanding that once you have conquered the storm which rages within, the storms which rage without can have little effect on you. In truth, the storm which rages within is the only storm over which you have power. The storm which rages without is beyond your influence but how you deal with it has much to do with whether or not you have conquered the storm within.

The yearly miracle of rebirth is reflected within the world around us. The miracle of the resurrection speaks to a greater truth, we are eternal and the death of the physical body announces only our rebirth into Spirit. While we mourn the loss of our loved ones from the physical, Spirit rejoices at their rebirth into the world of Spirit—the Heaven World. A world where they are freed from the limitations of the physical—a world of Light and truth—a world where they can rediscover their heritage. Our birth into the world of Spirit begins the cycle anew.

Cycles are important to our orderly universe. What cycles do you know in nature? The return of our spring flowers, the movement of Canada Geese overhead, and the certainty that spring follows winter. Cycles help us understand the order in our world. Cycles are predictable and their familiarity helps us function more comfortably even when faced with chaos.

Imagine a great bird which upon its death is consumed by a fire from within. From its own ashes, it arises again—renewed, rejuvenated, and refreshed. This is the phoenix, an ancient image arising from its own ashes. The ancients understood the cycles of birth and rebirth many thousands of years before Christ walked the earth. The resurrection of Christ reaffirms our understanding of the cycles of rebirth. It affirms our immortality.

This cycle is reflected in the natural world in many forms. The one which is probably most familiar to us all is that of the butterfly. It begins its life born from an egg in the form of a caterpillar. It lives a short life as a caterpillar going about its daily activities of survival unaware that it has a greater heritage—unaware of the door through which it must pass. As it spins its cocoon, it feels that it is nearly at the end of its existence and as it drifts into hibernation, indeed the existence it has known is over. When it awakes, it is transformed. For the once cumbersome caterpillar, a new life has begun as a beautiful, delicate butterfly, unrecognizable now from its previous form. So it is with our rebirth into Spirit. When we awaken after our transformation, we are no longer encumbered by the physical. We are in a world of thought where the concepts of time and space have little meaning. We have traveled to the Heaven World. As the butterfly soars, we now soar!

Another important cycle for those of us living on earth is that of the seasons. There are many types of seasons. In nature, we travel through the seasons of spring, summer, fall and winter. Each has its purpose. Each has its flavour and special character.

The seasons correspond to:

Spring	- the sowing of seed
	- birth
Summer	- a period of maturing and growth
Fall	- the harvest
Winter	- a fallow or rest period
Spring	- sowing of new improved seed
	- rebirth

If we look at our lives, we can see these seasons reflected. One way of understanding it is:

Spring	- preparation for birth into the physical
	- conception and birth
Summer	- living one's life—learning, growing
Fall	- harvest what we have sown
Winter	- death
Spring	- ebirth into Spirit
Summer	- period in spirit examining our former life
Spring	- preparation for rebirth into the physical
	- birth into the physical

Look around you. Learn to see the order—the cycles—the purposefulness which surrounds and enfolds our existence.

In an orderly universe, there must be natural laws. We have learned to understand some of the physical and spiritual laws which bring order. What are some of these natural laws?

We might express some of them as:

- We live in a free will universe. (That means we are the masters of our own fate)
- Thoughts are things. As you think, so it is.
- Everything happens for a reason and is purposeful.
- We reap what we sow.
- Like-minded souls have a tendency to gather together.
- There are many paths but one truth. Love is the ultimate power in the universe and stands supreme.
- Do all things through love.
- We are measured not by our deeds but by our thoughts.

Let us remind ourselves that we are eternal and that each of us will someday stand in the world of Spirit. Let us remind ourselves that the Christ and all the great masters have brought to us a message of love and Light. Let us remind ourselves that we can embrace the Light to prosper and grow. Each of us, whatever our tradition, is a child of the Light and is in search of truth.

May God bless each of you and help you move along your path to truth.

On the Topic of Miracles

What is a miracle? The dictionary defines a miracle as an act or event that seems to transcend or contradict all known natural or scientific laws and is usually thought of as supernatural in origin. A miracle is a wondrous event.

This is a good working definition. I believe, however, that miracles do follow natural laws. I also believe that they happen every day. We just do not recognize them or acknowledge them. We are trained not to. Isn't it true that people who believe in miracles are unrealistic and dreamers? Is it not true that people who believe in miracles do not have their feet on the ground? It is time we stopped being embarrassed because we have faith and believe in miracles.

Science tells us that there are scientific explanations for everything and that miraculous events do not occur. Science also told us that anti-matter could not exist. Well, anti-matter does exist. Science once told us that the smallest possible molecular particle was the atom. Well, it isn't. Science once said that people would never make it into outer space. Not only have people made it into space but we have walked on the moon. Science has discovered some of the natural laws, but other laws they have not discovered. Our knowledge of the world, both seen and unseen, changes with each day. With each new discovery, the way we understand the world changes.

There are those who are complacent and feel that we have reached the heights of our potential for achievement and reject change. This is the type of thinking that permits us to stop believing in miracles. We limit ourselves by the thinking of the day or what we know at that point. It is the arrogance of ignorance. It is the difference between linear thinking and non-linear thinking. It is the inability to accept that which you cannot see or understand. Did you know that there are actually people who think that man never actually made it to the moon?

Does science understand how we think and reason? No. Do we understand how consciousness begins? No. Can we create life? No. Does understanding something make it less miraculous? I can still look at many things I understand and see them as miraculous. These include the opening of a flower or the flight of a bee or life itself. These are wondrous things even when we believe that we understand them.

It would seem that some miracles are more "miraculous" than others. Miracles can be called many names: coincidence, luck and when healing occurs, we call it psychosomatic. No matter what the name, when for example spontaneous healing occurs, it is miraculous. A miracle is a miracle. A minor miracle is still a miracle.

There are other less flattering names that those who do not accept miracles call miraculous events. For those who have had near-death experiences, past-life experiences, visions, or seen apparitions, they will say hallucinations, imagination, hypnosis (and when a lot of people see it—it is a group hallucination or hysteria), delusions, brain cells dying and worse. Some may be the manifestations of a delusional mind but what of those experiences that are later found to be real and have their foundations in reality. Science would have us believe that miraculous events never happen. They are not being honest with us or themselves. Many experiences are later substantiated or have a foundation in fact.

Some who do not believe in miracles point to the fact that they can reproduce the event through trickery. This only proves that they cannot reproduce a miracle and must turn to trickery. It does not prove a miraculous event did not occur. People make counterfeit money and it imitates quite convincingly the real thing. Does that mean that real money does not exist?

The native Indians have a special name for God. They call God "The Great Mystery." I think this is a wonderful way to think of God because it speaks to the fact that God is incomprehensible and miraculous.

Miracles occur. There is proof. Why is it then that so few people accept the concrete evidence that God is there? There are many reasons and today we can't discuss them all but we can talk about one. Many people seem to think that if a miracle can't be produced on demand then it is no good. I thought that was what a miracle was—something that happens unexpectedly and cannot be reproduced on demand. Not that everyday things like a seed growing into a flower and the laughter of children aren't miracles, they are—but healings, visitations, prophesies and other manifestations of God's power happen through the grace of God, and not because we have placed an order for a miracle. They cannot be studied using the traditional scientific method for they are, by definition not reproducible and beyond the understanding of science. THEY ARE MIRACLES!!

When asking for a miracle, we must always be sure that we add to our request, "As it is for my (or their) own best good." It is not our place to decide what is right for someone else. We should never impose absolutes upon our request for help and guidance. We do not know the journey that others must take nor the trials through which they must pass. We must ask for healing or a miracle but always leave the final choice to those receiving the gift and to God. We must give God the freedom to shape events in the way that will work for our greater purpose. That is part of the price of free will.

A few years ago I was talking to a healer from Mexico. He shared an experience he had while doing a healing for the father of a family. He had been called to do a healing by the wife of a man who had a brain aneurysm and had been told that he only had a short time to live. He arrived and met the mother and the two children and was taken to the man who was unconscious in an adjacent room. He began the healing and Spirit told him they could not heal this man. He began again and was told again that the man would not be healed. The healer protested that this man had a family and that the man was needed to support his wife and children. Again he was told that the miracle would not happen. In desperation, the healer said," For me, please heal this man. "Spirit said, "For you, we will heal him." Over the next week, the man made a miraculous recovery and regained his health. The healer was overjoyed and went on with his life.

About a year later, the healer was reading the paper when he saw the picture of the man he had healed. The caption over the picture read something like—"MAN DIES IN PRISON." The healer immediately went to the house where the family of the man he had healed lived and knocked on the door. The door was answered by the grandmother. The healer showed her the newspaper and asked what had happened.

The grandmother explained with tears in her eyes that the man had lost his temper and killed his wife who was her daughter. He had quite a temper and was prone to violence. After he had gone to prison for murder, he had gotten into a fight and had himself been killed by an inmate. The healer was devastated and gave the grandmother his condolences and went home.

At home, he asked Spirit, "Why did this happen? I do not understand." Spirit replied, "We had told you the man should not be healed. Better that one should die than two."

In the case of this healer, even though the healer could perform a miracle through his will, he did not have the faith to trust that the choice already made was the right one even though it would leave the family without a father. It was a difficult lesson for him to learn and one which had a great cost.

The Bible gives us many examples of miracles. There are events such as the parting of the Red Sea, the feeding of the multitude, walking on water, the healing of the sick, visions and apparitions and many, many, more. There are miracles attributed to the saints. Yet today, you hear very little about miracles. When you do, it is often with an air of suspicion that they are mentioned.

Experts tell us how these miracles could be faked with technology. Is it so hard to believe that God is working in our lives today? Have we become so cynical and blinded that even when we have proof, we must reject it?

It is true that there is deception in the world and that all the miracles you hear about are not necessarily real or true (especially if you read the tabloids). But we must approach the topic with an open mind and let the facts speak for themselves. Never assume miracles do not and cannot happen in your life.

It is the right of every soul while on earth to have everything they need in order to live a fulfilling life. This fact has been demonstrated to us time and again. Moses led the Israelites into the desert without food or water and the people were fearful. But their needs were always met.

People, it seems have always been sceptical of that which is not under their control. "You can't expect a miracle" is the phrase we have been programmed with for most of our lives. We pride ourselves on modern technology and on our ability to adapt as new discoveries are unearthed. Why then do we still feel that if we do not understand it, it cannot be valid? Do you understand how an atomic power plant works or a satellite or your microwave?

Brother Andre, the small illiterate but very Spiritual and dedicated religious brother of the Roman Catholic Order, spent many years of his life in a healing ministry. He had the gift of healing and many times was assailed by those within his own order as well as those from other walks of life. He persevered, and because of that thousands, including medical doctors and clergy, witnessed the miraculous healings he accomplished. Arriving in wheelchairs and on crutches, people got up and walked away. These people believed in miracles. People still come today to Montreal to visit his tomb and ask for a miracle. The crutches of the healed cover the walls and you know—miracles still happen there today even though Brother Andre has been dead for many years.

In June, 1984 at a college campus in Minnesota, a young blind lady presented herself for healing to Reverend Marilyn Rossner, President and Founder of the SSF Interfaith Ministry. Tayja Wiger's condition had deteriorated since birth and when she arrived for the service she was considered legally blind by the state. She was accompanied by a seeing-eye-dog. The reaction among the 500 people in attendance was tumultuous when after praying and healing by the laying-on-of-hands, Tayja began to scream, "I can see! I can see!" In a subsequent letter from one of Minnesota's leading ophthalmologist who, on behalf of the State, regularly examined Tayja wrote "I am pleased to report that I have re-examined Ms. Wiger, July 17, 1984 and have discovered she has regained all her sight with the aid of a Spiritual healer . . ." Today Tayja is a minister in the Interfaith Ministry.

Miracles do happen today. Think back to the miracles in your life. Think back to the things which have brought you insight and understanding. Think back to the things that have brought you to where you are today. Accept God in your life and allow God's Light to bring you joy and comfort.

When you are in need, pray to the God of your understanding. Speak out loud. There is no need for rash promises. Just ask. God knows what you need but to allow you to exercise your free will, you must ask. God wants you to be happy. Oh yes! And expect a miracle!

The Paths are Many, the Truth is One

Now there are varieties of gifts, but the same Spirit; and there are varieties of service, but the same Lord; and there are varieties of working, but it is the same God who inspires them all in every one. To each is given the manifestation of the Spirit for the common good.

Christianity.

Bible, 1 Corinthians 12.4-7

Many Paths, One Truth

Recently someone asked me, if there is one God then why are there so many religions? This is a very fair question.

People who have grown up in or have had exposure to only one tradition have very little information to work with, because they have an understanding of only one perspective. They ask the questions "How can one have an Interfaith Ministry?" If there is one God, then isn't it obvious that there must be one true religion to worship that God? How can there be many paths to God? The other religions do not believe what we believe."

Today, I am going to explore these questions.

First, let's look at the idea that there are many paths to God. In an Interfaith Ministry, we state it as, "There are Many Paths but One Truth, Love thy Neighbour." Just what do the great religious traditions think of this idea?

The scriptures of each religion contain passages which recognize that there are truths in other paths. They recognize that the teachings and practices of other faiths may be similar in many respects to their own. Even though it is not always practised by the faithful, all scriptures teach tolerance and respect for righteous and sincere believers of other faiths. There is no place for intolerance and egoism in religion.

There are various scriptures which affirm that others who do not share the faith of that scripture are also following the way of Truth. Thus

Hinduism, Jainism and Buddhism understand the various deities to be expressions of a single Absolute Reality, and the various paths to lead to one Supreme Goal. Judaism has the doctrine of the Noahic laws, God's revelation to all humankind through which non-Jews can be righteous before God. The Christian Bible contains passages affirming that God had intimated himself in the religion of the Greeks. Sikhism affirms the common spiritual origin of Islam and Hinduism. The Islamic scriptures affirm that Jews and Christians are "people of the book" who share the same God as the God of Muhammad. It is also true that many religions teach that a non-believer, if he or she does righteousness, is acceptable before God.

I would like to share with you a few excerpt from various scriptures which illustrate the principle of many paths, one truth.

> *As men approach Me, so I receive them. All paths, Arjuna, lead to Me. Hinduism. Bhagavad Gita 4.11*

> *They have called him Indra, Mitra, Varuna, Agni, and the divine fine-winged Garuda; They speak of Indra, Yama, Matrarisvan: the One Being sages call by many names. Hinduism. Rig Veda 1.164.46*

> *Confucius said . . . "In the world there are many different roads but the destination is the same. There are a hundred deliberations but the result is one." Confucianism. I Ching, Appended Remarks 2.5*

> *At any time, in any form and accepted name, if one is shorn of all attachment, that one is you alone. My Lord! You are one although variously appearing. Jainism. Hemachandra, Dvatrimshika 20*

Buddha explains that he has assumed various human forms in countless different worlds to guide every possible being to the right path.

> *The Buddha declared to the bodhisattva Aksayamati, "To those who can be conveyed to deliverance by the body of an elder . . . a*

householder . . . an official . . . a woman . . . a boy or girl . . . a god, dragon, spirit, angel, demon, garuda-bird, centaur, serpent, human or non-human, he preaches Dharma by displaying the appropriate body . . . . The bodhisattva Avalokitesvara, by resorting to a variety of forms, travels the world, conveying the beings to salvation." Buddhism. Lotus Sutra 25

The Qur'an teaches that Muhammad is one of a succession of true prophets who have given God's message to diverse peoples; cf. *Islam. Qur'an 4.163-65, p. 663, and 19.41-58, p.665.*

Verily We have sent messengers before you, among them some of those of whom We have told you, and some of whom We have not told you. Islam. Qur'an 40.78

Say, "We believe in God, and in what has been revealed to us, and what was revealed to Abraham, Ishmael, Isaac, Jacob, and the Tribes, and in what was given to Moses, Jesus, and the Prophets from their Lord. We make no distinction between any of them, and to God do we submit. Islam. Qur'an 3.84

Those who believe in the Qur'an, those who follow the Jewish scriptures, and the Sabeans and the Christians—any who believe in God and the Last Day, and work righteousness—on them shall be no fear, nor shall they grieve. Islam. Qur'an 5.69

And unto thee, We revealed the Scripture with the truth, confirming whatever Scripture was before it, and a watcher over it. So judge between them by that which God has revealed, and follow not their desires apart from the truth which has come unto thee. For each, We have appointed a divine law and a traced-out way. Had God willed He could have made you one community. But that He may try you by that which He has given you, He made you as you are. So vie one with another in good works. Unto God you will all return, and He will then inform you of that wherein you differ. Islam. Qur'an 5.44, 46-48

Rabbi Joshua said, "There are righteous men among the nations who have a share in the world to come." Judaism. Tosefta Sanhedrin 13.2

Since the children of Noah are the ancestors of all humankind, the rabbis have traditionally interpreted these laws, given by God to Noah after the flood in Genesis 9.3-7, as moral legislation given by God to all nations. By obeying these laws, a Gentile is accounted righteous before God. Judaism. Tosefta Sanhedrin 56a

And I [Jesus] have other sheep, that are not of this fold; I must bring them also, and they will heed my voice. So there shall be one flock, one shepherd. Christianity. Bible, John 10.16

So Paul, standing in the middle of the Areopagus, said, "Men of Athens, I perceive that in every way you are very religious. For as I passed along, and observed the objects of your worship, I found also an altar with this inscription, 'To an unknown god.' What therefore you worship as unknown, this I proclaim to you. The God who made the world and everything in it, being Lord of heaven and earth, does not live in shrines made by man, nor is he served by human hands, as though he needed anything, since he himself gives to all men life and breath and everything. And he made from one every nation of men to live on the face of the earth, having determined allotted periods and the boundaries of their habitation, that they should seek God, in the hope that they might feel after him and find him. Yet he is not far from each one of us, for 'In him we live and move and have our being'; as even some of your poets have said, 'For we are indeed his offspring.'" Christianity. Bible, Acts 17.22-28

When one begins to embrace the concept that there are many paths but one truth, there is another conclusion that follows. It is that there is one God and that one God has become manifest to many peoples in different forms. This one God is the foundation of all religions. All religions are connected to the same Ultimate reality leading people towards a common goal.

In Hermetic Philosophy which is believed to have been handed down from the time of early Egypt, the God Source is called THE ALL and is considered unknowable, eternal, and infinite. THE ALL is seen as the Substantial Reality—the Fundamental Truth which is under, and back of the Universe of Time, Space and Change.

In the Kybalion it states, *"THE ALL must be ALL that really is. There can be nothing existing outside of THE ALL, else THE ALL would not be THE ALL."* It goes on to state that, *"THE ALL must be INFINITE, for there is nothing else to define, confine, bound, limit or restrict THE ALL. It must be INFINITE in Time—ETERNAL.*

I find this notion of THE ALL compelling for its simplicity and its similarity to the GOD embraced by the world's religious traditions. No matter what name you choose to give God, God in all traditions is infinite and absolute, and there can be only one. To illustrate this, let us look at how the different traditions describe God. If the God they describe has the same or similar qualities, then it must be the same God they are talking about.

> *I am the Lord, and there is no other, besides me there is no God. Judaism and Christianity—Bible, Isaiah 45.5*

> *Say, He is God, the One! God, the eternally Besought of all! He neither begets nor was begotten. And there is none comparable unto Him. Islam. Qur'an 112*

> *He is the one God, hidden in all beings, all-pervading, the Self within all beings, watching over all works, dwelling in all beings, the witness, the perceiver, the only one, free from qualities. Hinduism. Svetasvatara Upanishad 6.11*

> *He is the Sole Supreme Being; of eternal manifestation; Creator, Immanent Reality; Without Fear, Without Rancor; Timeless Form; Unincarnated; Self-existent; Realized by the grace of the Holy Preceptor. Sikhism. Adi Granth, Japuji, p. 1: The Mul Mantra*

Absolute truth is indestructible. Being indestructible, it is eternal. Being eternal, it is self-existent. Being self-existent, it is infinite. Being infinite, it is vast and deep. Being vast and deep, it is transcendental and intelligent. It is because it is vast and deep that it contains all existence. It is because it is transcendental and intelligent that it embraces all existence. It is because it is infinite and eternal that it fulfils or perfects all existence. In vastness and depth it is like the Earth. In transcendental intelligence it is like Heaven. Infinite and eternal, it is the Infinite itself. Such being the nature of absolute truth, it manifests itself without being seen; it produces effects without motion; it accomplishes its ends without action. Confucianism. Doctrine of the Mean 26

When we look at the ways that God is described in the different traditions, it is easy to see that they are all talking about one eternal, singular entity. Even the traditions which have many deities worship one God which has many manifestations which are represented by different deities. Some traditions, such as the Baha'i faith state it clearly:

There can be no doubt that whatever the peoples of the world, of whatever race or religion, derive their inspiration from one heavenly Source, and are the subjects of one God. The difference between the ordinances under which they abide should be attributed to the varying requirements and exigencies of the age in which they were revealed. All of them, except for a few which are the outcomes of human perversity, were ordained of God, and are a reflection of His Will and Purpose. Baha'i Faith. Gleanings from the Writings of Baha'u'llah 111

The Buddhist state:

When appearances and names are put away and all discrimination ceases, that which remains is the true and essential nature of things and, as nothing can be predicated as to the nature of essence, is called the "Suchness" of Reality. This universal, undifferentiated, inscrutable Suchness is the only Reality, but it is variously characterized as Truth, Mind-essence,

Transcendental Intelligence, Perfection of Wisdom, etc. This Dharma of the imagelessness of the Essence-nature of Ultimate Reality is the Dharma which has been proclaimed by all the Buddhas, and when all things are understood in full agreement with it, one is in possession of Perfect Knowledge. Buddhism. Lankavatara Sutra

In the Bible, we read that God is found in every land:

For from the rising of the sun to its setting my name is great among the nations, and in every place incense is offered to my name, and a pure offering; for my name is great among the nations, says the Lord of hosts. Judaism and Christianity. Bible, Malachi 1.11

The Bible also notes that there is one God for all.

Now there are varieties of gifts, but the same Spirit; and there are varieties of service, but the same Lord; and there are varieties of working, but it is the same God who inspires them all in every one. To each is given the manifestation of the Spirit for the common good. Christianity. Bible, 1 Corinthians 12.4-7

God said to Israel, "Because you have seen me in many likenesses, there are not therefore many gods. But it is ever the same God: I am the Lord your God." Rabbi Levi said, "God appeared to them like a mirror, in which many faces can be reflected; a thousand people look at it; it looks at all of them." So when God spoke to the Israelites, each one thought that God spoke individually to him. Judaism. Midrash, Pesikta Kahana 109b-110a.

Look at the world around you. Isn't the world we live in filled with great diversity and beauty? There is not just one type of bird, or one type of flower or one type of tree or one type of person. The world is filled with thousands of myriad forms which are birds, flowers, trees, and people. God is a God of diversity. This diversity allows us to see the many manifestations which can be birds, and flowers and people.

A God of diversity would not have but one face. God has many faces and appears to different peoples in different forms through different traditions.

We as an Interfaith community accept the truth that there is one God—a God of Love. We accept that this one God has manifested to different cultures and peoples through different prophets and faiths throughout the ages. We believe that there are many paths but one truth. We celebrate and rejoice at the many faces God has shown us. We celebrate and rejoice that we are all children of the one Light.

About the Author

Rev. Barry King
B.Sc.(Hon.), Ph.D.(T.C.), OM, n.d.,
Reiki Master and OIIM RSPchmd
Master Spiritual Medium

Rev. Barry is a true Renaissance man whose rich background includes over forty years of experience as a museum professional and educator. His other diverse roles include naturalist, artist, illustrator, author, editor, intuitive, counsellor and Interfaith Minister. A pioneer in the Interfaith/Interspiritual Movement for over thirty years, he has dedicated his life to a path of spiritual growth and service. Rev Barry and his wife, Rev. Sandi, are the co-founders of the Prince Edward Island Interfaith Ministry, the Open International Interfaith Ministry (OIIM) and its Interfaith seminary, the iNtuitive Times Institute.

Having a strong connection to Spirit since birth, Rev Barry has worked to develop his intuitive gifts. He has committed himself to sharing the certain knowledge that there is no death and that we are all Spirit. He has an active practice in spiritual readings and consultations and is well-known as a proof of survival medium. In his work as a Spiritual Medium, Interfaith Spiritual Counsellor, Spiritual Healer, and Spiritual Director, he helps clients develop their own connection and receive guidance from the Divine Source. Rev. Barry is a Reiki Master and a registered Naturotherapist with the Academy of Naturopaths and Naturotherapists (A.N.N.). He has also been awarded the OIIM Registration Board's title Master Spiritual Medium.

Through the Interfaith Ministry, Rev. Barry helps to provide a safe, respectful and reverent environment for exploring spirituality and shares the knowledge that intuitive abilities are Gifts of Spirit and as such, everyone's birthright.

For more information contact Rev Barry King at:

www.interfaithministry.com
www.revbarryking.ca